Whitman® Juvenile Books

Reference & Value Guide

David and Virginia Brown

COLLECTOR BOOKS

A Division of Schroeder Publishing Co., Inc.

Whitman Publishing Company is a subsidiary of Western Publishing Company.

Whitman®, Big Little Books®, Better Little Books™, and Trixie Belden® are trademarks of Golden Books Publishing Company, Inc., used with permission. The current values in this book should be used only as a guide. They are not intended to set prices, which vary from one section of the country to another. Auction prices as well as dealer prices vary greatly and are affected by condition as well as demand. Neither the Authors nor the Publisher assumes responsibility for any losses that might be incurred as a result of consulting this guide.

Photographs by Virginia Brown

Cover design: Terri Stalions
Book design: Joyce Cherry

Searching For A Publisher?

We are always looking for knowledgeable people considered to be experts within their fields. If you feel that there is a real need for a book on your collectible subject and have a large comprehensive collection, contact Collector Books.

On the Cover:
LASSIE And the Mystery at Blackberry Bog – $14.00
FIVE LITTLE PEPPERS And How They Grew – $6.00
TRIXIE BELDEN® And The Mystery on the Mississippi – $5.00
ROBINSON CRUSOE – $10.00
RED RYDER And The Secret of the Lucky Mine – $20.00
BAT MASTERSON – $15.00
LITTLE WOMEN – $16.00
POLLY FRENCH And The Surprising Stranger – $6.00
HEIDI – $4.00
GENE AUTRY And The Golden Ladder Gang – $25.00

COLLECTOR BOOKS
P.O. Box 3009
Paducah, Kentucky 42002-3009

Copyright © 1997 David and Virginia Brown

Values Updated, 1999

Contents

Acknowledgments

I would like to extend my gratitude and appreciation to the following persons and organizations that helped make this book possible: to Ginny Brown for assistance and support in countless ways; to Alana Brown for her patience, acceptance, and belief; to Mary Anderson for her enthusiasm and assistance in acquiring titles; to the State Historical Society of Wisconsin for their invaluable help with reference materials; to the Porter Memorial Library for their active interest in the project; to the Antiquarian Booksellers Associations of Maine, New Hampshire, Massachusetts, and Rhode Island; and to all the sellers and collectors who gladly gave of their time and experience.

About the Authors

David G. Brown is the training director for the county jail in Washington County, Maine. He is on the Board of Trustees of the Porter Memorial Library and is active in local politics. Together with his wife, Ginny, they own and operate a mobile home park and an on-line antiques shop, Cybertiques. They reside in Machias, Maine, with their daughter, Alana. They are presently working on a companion volume to this one. They may be reached at cybertiques@nemaine.com.

History Of Whitman Publishing

The Whitman Publishing Company is a wholly owned subsidiary of the Western Printing & Lithographing Company. The parent company was founded in 1907 by Edward H. Wadewitz, who died in January 1955. During his 48 years at the helm, the firm increased enormously. The firm's primary business is printing but it does much more than just that.

The company that was to become the Western Printing and Lithographing Company began in 1905 as the West Side Printing Company located in the basement of the Dr. Fazen Building in the 600 block of State Street in Racine, Wisconsin. Run by John Geller, it was a Gordon shop, doing small job work. One of the employees was a boy just out of school, William Wadewitz, about whom we will hear more shortly.

In 1906, Edward H. Wadewitz was a young man working as a bank employee who had been sent to investigate the possibilities of liquidating the print shop troubled by financial difficulties. As he examined the shop, he decided that he was interested in printing. Geller sold his interest in the shop to the young banker and he began his new career with capital of less than $1,500. Early in 1907, Wadewitz formed a partnership with William Bell, who had been employed by the Journal Printing Company as a journeyman pressman. Three months later, Roy A. Spencer, who was also an employee of Journal Printing, came aboard as a third partner. Before the year was out, Bell sold his interest to the other partners.

That first year, business for the West Side Printing Company amounted to only $5,000 but the Company still managed to turn a profit. The employees at the time were Edward H. Wadewitz, Roy A. Spencer, W.R. Wadewitz, William Williams, and Kate Bongarts. By 1908, business had grown to $8,000; in 1910, it leaped to $19,000; and by 1914, business had increased to a credible $127,000. It was in 1915 that the lithographic department was added and the name of the West Side Printing Company was changed to the Western Printing and Lithographing Company, or the "Western" as it came to be known in-house. Up until this time, the company had only been doing commercial printing. Some of its commercial accounts were S.C. Johnson & Son, J.I. Case Plow Works Company, the Signal Shirt Company, and the Harvey Spring Company. Because of the large volume of commercial work, the company found that it was hard to keep a steady volume of work going through the plant. They discovered that it was either feast or famine since they had no fillers of any sort.

Then Western began to seek filler work that could be done when commercial work ebbed. One of those accounts was the printing and binding work of a line of juvenile books for the Hamming-Whitman Publishing Company of Chicago. For the first year or so, the account was very good. The book publishers paid their bills and met their commitments as they increased their line. Unfortunately, their working capital was insufficient to meet the sudden increase in demand for their products and the publishing company found itself in financial distress. Hamming-Whitman was forced into bankruptcy. Because of his background in banking and his experience in overseeing bankruptcies, Edward Wadewitz was appointed to the creditor's committee. The business ran for a year under his management and then was taken over from the creditors by the Western and the Whitman Publishing Company was born. For the next two years or so, the Western continued with the previous line of medium- to high-priced books which were sold to book and department stores. Western also got in touch with some of Hamming-Whitman's business connections. During this period only a few new books were added.

In 1918, the Western received its first order from the syndicate field, from the Kresge Stores. The company was ecstatic that they had received such a huge order. It was this first order that launched the Whitman Publishing Company into the forefront of the children's book field, although not for the reasons one might think. Paper was purchased and stockpiled to fill the huge order and the books went to press. Only then did someone discover that the original order had been misread and that it in fact only called for one-fifth the quantity that it was thought to contain. An employee named Sam Lowe averted disaster and forged the future path of Whitman® by going out and selling the overproduced books to Woolworth and other syndicates. Up to this time, the syndicates had not paid much attention to children's books. They carried only a basic line of classic titles. Lowe managed to convince the syndicates that a market existed for new and original books. He operated on the premise that "nothing was too good to go into the 10 cent line." This market increased in volume until it grew to such proportions that it became necessary to put a man with working knowledge of the different operations in charge.

Thus, William Wadewitz, the schoolboy from Geller's print shop, came to head this filler operation that had in turn become a large part of the Western's volume. This was no small task since at Whitman® Publishing Company in 1929 more than 200 items were being produced, comprising more than 14 million books and 1.5 million games. Together with Whitman®, the Western grew to a point at which they reached an annual sales volume of $80 million by 1957. Behind these figures was a physical plant with facilities in Racine, Wisconsin; Poughkeepsie, New York; St. Louis and Hannibal, Missouri; and Mount Morris, Illinois, as well as sales offices in New York City, Beverly Hills, Atlanta, Detroit, Boston, Chicago, Minneapolis, Dallas, and San Francisco, with editorial offices in New York City and a steady work force of some 4,700 employees.

This book concerns itself with the books for children published by the Whitman® Publishing Company, specifically with the 8" books known as 50-cent juveniles. Other sizes were tried at various times as well, but the 8vo (octavo) or 8"–9" format is predominant. Most collectors have been aware for some time now of the Big Little Books® published by Whitman® as well as the Better Little Books™. Their size and cartoonish aspects made them attractive items to many collectors. Additionally, there were many persons who remembered them from their own childhood who were interested in them for sentimental reasons. Those are covered in depth in other publications, a notable one by Dale

Manesis and another by Larry Jacobs, *Big Little Books – A Collector's Reference & Value Guide* (Collector Books, 1996).

In addition to books, Whitman® published a wide range of board games, jigsaw puzzles, paper doll books, coloring books, and other childhood ephemera. 1995 marks the eightieth year since Whitman® Books began publishing children's books. During that time, hundreds of books targeting a variety of young audiences have been printed. The juveniles were published in a variety of series: Whitman® Classics, Adventures for Boys, Mysteries, and others. The most notable series, however, was the Authorized Editions. These books were gleaned from radio, screen, and comic strips and the stories revolved around personalities engaged in stories of adventure, mystery or humor. Later, the authorized versions were expanded to include the stars of well-known TV series of the '50s, '60s, and '70s. Many stories were published repeatedly under a variety of covers. Early versions had plain covers with dust jackets on which the main characters were illustrated or photographed. In the '50s, illustrated or photograph covers with a laminated coating became the norm. It is possible to find many books in both a plain cover version and in a laminated cover version. Also, many of the titles that were published in laminated form were re-published in later years with different artwork on the cover.

Today we take for granted the concept of licensing. Companies submit bids to the holder of a license to produce clothing, toys, and other merchandise, and to publish books and records, as well as thousands of other items that may bear little or no relation to the original license except for the fact that they are now produced with a title or logo. We have recently witnessed the explosion of merchandise associated with the Teenage Mutant Ninja Turtles™ where thousands of items were produced. Similarly, the Batman® movies have spawned truckloads of associated items. There was a time when licensing and licensed products were relatively sparse. Sometimes an advertiser would pick up on a subject to associate with their product, such as Outcault's Buster Brown or the Katzenjammer Kids, but not to the degree we see today. Whitman® Publishing with their books, puzzles, games, cards, and other printed materials depended in large degree on the licenses they could acquire.

Over the years, Whitman® entered into

numerous deals with the owners of characters and the agents of personalities. Because of these extensive licensing arrangements, their books provide a wide-ranging snapshot of popular culture from the 1920s to the 1970s. Many of the characters chosen remain icons today. Some of the subjects chosen for licensing by Whitman® were of less than enduring popularity; others are positively obscure. But this is one of the attractions of the Whitman® line. Through this medium, these lesser lights of another age remain alive. Someone at some time knew and cared about these characters and personalities who in some small way helped to shape an age and a world. Whitman® books were contemporary with comic books and the subject matter that they both addressed was comparable. However, these books had, and continued to have, their niche in that they were interesting to children yet parents could rest easy knowing that their children were actually reading and not just looking at pictures. There was another aspect of popular culture that ran parallel to and contributed to the phenomenon of Whitman® Books. These were the Saturday matinee movies. The strings of serials shown at these events were similar both in content and the level of excitement and adventure offered to young viewers and readers.

As is the case in any successful venture, Whitman® faced stiff competition for portions of the market share. Some of their competitors for the youth market were Saalfield Publishing Company, M.A. Donahue & Company, A.L. Burt Company, Grossett & Dunlap, Goldsmith Publishing, Triangle Books, and Cupples & Leon Company All of them published books in a similar vein to those produced by Whitman® and there were many occasions when the same title would be produced by several publishers.

Collector's Information

A sign of the regard in which these little books were held is the number of books that turn up with inscriptions inside the cover. It is unusual to find a book that does not have a memorial of "Christmas 1946", or "To Annie, From Grampie and Grannie", or a similar note from Uncle Dinghy. Another attractive aspect of the Whitman® books is the relative ease with which they can be obtained. Sometimes they are still offered by the original owners at yard and garage sales for 25 or 50 cents. Nearly all book and antiques dealers have some quantity stashed away somewhere. It is not supply that is daunting, but rather the sheer number of titles that is available. There are few times when I go out looking that I do not discover some title, series, or variation of which I was not aware. That is not to say that there aren't titles that are scarce, or even rare. There are. There are also titles that you trip over every time you turn around.

The Whitman® line meets all the essential qualifications for a collectible. It was created in great numbers and variety, was affordable to a wide range of purchasers, was (and is) considered "disposable" by a great many, and has a high degree of crossover. By crossover I mean that the subject matter of the book ties in to the interests of other collectors in different areas. For instance, a Walt Disney's Annette book may appeal to a Disney collector, a fan of Annette Funicello, an aficionado of beach movies, or a latter day Mouseketeer. Considering that most of the Whitman® books dealt with radio, movie, TV or comic personalities, the crossover potential is enormous.

There are many factors on which a collection can be based. Author, subject, genre, and cover artist are some of the more common criteria. As your collection grows, you will need to think about specializing. There are no hard and fast rules to guide you in making acquisitions. As in all transactions, there must be a willing seller and a willing buyer. If the item in question is desirable and the price is acceptable, then buy it. However, you will want to consider the relative scarcity of the book and/or its condition relative to the price. Obviously an otherwise common book in very fine condition with a dust jacket also in very fine condition will command some sort of premium. The first thing that should come to mind when deciding upon a purchase is condition. A common book with lam lift, a broken spine, and loose frontispiece may be fine at $1.00. But many dealers will put a price on it of $5.00 or $10.00 because they once saw a similar type of book go for that much. No matter that the other book was in nearly pristine condition or was a much older or rarer specimen. The dealer is in the business of selling to make a profit. They will charge whatever they think the market will bear. You are the one who must be an informed buyer. Carry in your mind an image of a perfect book — one with no flaws, as fresh and crisp as the day it was printed. Compare the books you see with that image. Then ask yourself if you are willing to pay the price asked for the product you are offered. The second thing that you should keep in mind is scarcity. If you have never seen the book offered before, then you may want to consider acquiring it on the basis that you might not encounter another copy. Some books were not terrifically popular when they were published or the target audience was one that was particularly hard on books. Another limitation is the lifespan of the program or character that spawned the series. Many of the shows on which TV books were based did not survive past a year or two at best. Needless to say, when the show died, so did the rationale for publishing the book. On the other hand, a title based on a long-running show may be scarce because there is a high demand for it from a broad spectrum of collectors. Either circumstance will tend to drive up the value of the particular book. Finally, you need to know what it is that you want from the book. If the cover art is what interests you, then you may not care if the text is scribbled with crayon. Conversely, if you are only interested in the text, then lam lift on the binding may not be of concern to you.

Another area of concern to the collector is how to properly care for and store their books. As a rule, books should always be stored in the upright position, that is, as they would sit on a shelf. Books that are laid flat can warp or the glue that holds the binding to the spine of the book can break. The two greatest enemies of your books are light and moisture. You should try to select a shelf that is not exposed to the direct light of the sun. Light will bleach out colors, rob paper of its strength and/or cause it to turn yellow. Books must never be stored in a damp location which will foster the growth of mildew and promote the health of vermin which may attack or even destroy your books. The ideal year-round humidity level is 50 percent. Too high a humidity level encourages the growth of fungus. Too low a humidity will cause the glue and paper to dry out and become brittle.

Defects

Some of the defects that you will encounter in your search for Whitman® books are:

Scuffing – This may range from a superficial abrasion of the cover to wear that goes through the cover to expose the cardboard underneath.

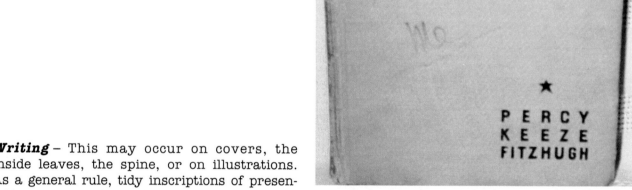

Writing – This may occur on covers, the inside leaves, the spine, or on illustrations. As a general rule, tidy inscriptions of presentation or ownership will only minimally effect the value. Messy writing, pricing, scribbling or doodling will have a more serious impact.

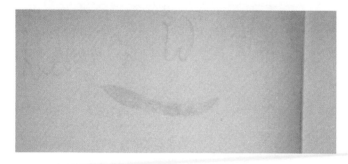

Sticker Pull – This refers to a discoloration or removal of color or material caused by pulling off a sticker. The presence of an original sticker in good condition does not detract from the value of the book. In the case of a promotional piece, the sticker is essential since it is the only means of identifying the promotion.

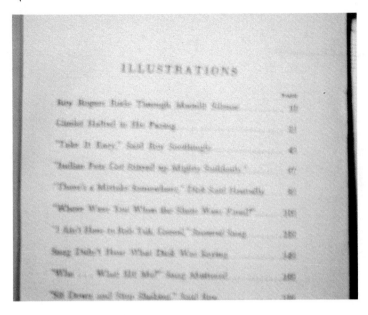

Darkening – This condition occurs when the book is stored in an acidic or dirty environment. The paper darkens and becomes brittle. Exposure to strong sunlight will hasten the process.

Fading – Usually effects the spine or the cover and is the result of direct sunlight or strong artificial light bleaching color from the cover. This can occur in a surprisingly short period of time.

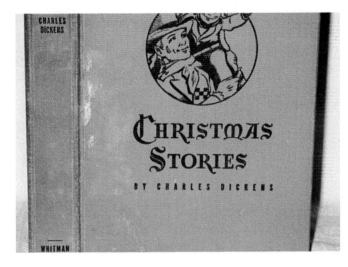

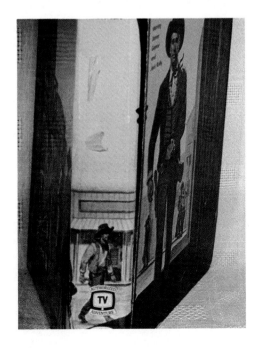

Lam Peel – Lam is short for lamination. The lam is the clear plastic film used to protect the illustrated covers of books produced from the '50s on. On some books the lamination has been abused or has become brittle. It then has a tendency to lift but should remain fairly stable if carefully handled.

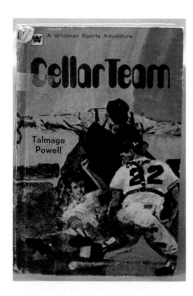

Tape Repair – This is a serious defect. Most tapes will eventually discolor and damage the paper or the book in the process.

Spine Split – This occurs when the spine is weakened by repeated use, dropping or bending back the covers. It usually occurs between the front cover and the first page but will occasionally happen with the back cover or the interior.

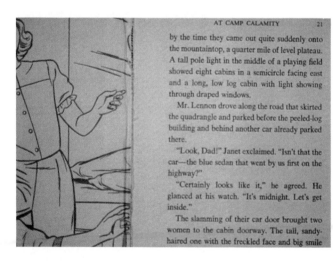

Missing or Loose Pages – Obviously this is a serious defect. Any such problem needs to be noted in any description of the book.

Cover Lift – This happens either when the book is bound too tightly or when the book has been subjected to moisture and then severely dried. The result is that the front cover will not lie flat.

Not Pictured

Cup Rings – Occurs when someone sets a sweaty glass on the book or uses it as a coaster. Very similar to the rings that glasses will leave on tables.

Grading Your Books

One of the most important considerations to collectors is the condition or grade of the item they collect. Since books are subject to continuous use ranging from gentle to brutal, condition becomes critical in assessing value. Just because a book has one or more flaws does not mean that it is completely valueless.

A book with missing pages will still have use to a collector interested in covers. A book without a cover may still have value for a reader. But they will never be as valuable as they would if they were in mint condition. Books are usually graded as follows:

Fine – Books in this category possess no flaws whatsoever and there is no indication that they have ever been read. In as-issued condition.

Near Fine – To the casual observer, these books will appear to be perfect. Close examination may reveal 2 or 3 small flaws. Generally, no scuffing, lam lift, or writing beyond a neat inscription. The spine is tight, colors fresh and the paper is white.

Very Good – Shows some signs that the book has been handled but no serious defects. No tears, stains or discoloration on either the binding or the dust jacket.

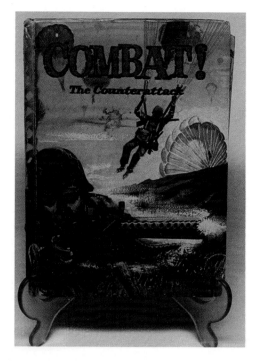

Good – Average used book. May have small tears and other defects. Has all of its pages. Some page corners may be dog-eared, slight flaking of the lamination at stress points and corners may be present. Wear is obvious. Perhaps some pencil marks and some loosening of the spine.

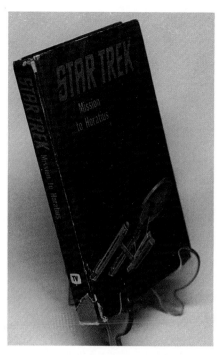

Reading Copy – Well worn but intact and complete. Shows signs of heavy use. Tape repairs, doodling, coloring, or scribbling may be present as long as the page is not obliterated. Major defects. Text must be complete.

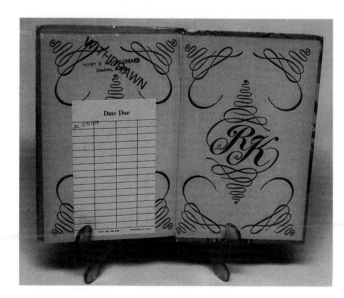

Ex-Library (Ex-Lib) – Should always be noted as such. May be encountered in any condition.

Some dealers may use other systems. Some may follow a term with plus or minus to indicate gradations. Others may use a numeric system with 10 as the highest descriptor. Their terms may differ, but the idea remains the same as outlined above.

In grading your books you must try to be as impartial as possible though this is sometimes very difficult. People have a tendency to grade the books in their collection higher than they actually are and to grade the books that they are considering for their collection lower than they are. Just because you choose to ignore a separated spine on your favorite book doesn't mean that anyone else will. What you see is what is there. Ignoring the flaw or wishing it away is pointless. While it is true that some rare or highly valued books are still expensive in a lesser condition, that value is always in comparison to a copy in better condition. If you have a difference of opinion with a seller as to the condition, be prepared to point out the specific defect to which you take exception.

Conventions

Each book listing contains some or all of the following elements:

Book Title – This is the main title of the book. Where "the" or "a" is the first word of the title, it has been moved to the end of the title to facilitate alphabetizing.

Story Title – This is the subtitle of the book.

Volume # – This number is found on the spine or back cover of all but the earliest books.

Copyright Date – This is the year of publication as noted in the book. Where there is no date, the entry "n.d." is used.

Author's Name – Listed with last name first, this is the person who actually wrote or adapted the book to this format. Where more than one author wrote stories for a collection, the authors are identified as "Various."

Cover – This indicates whether the cover is plain or illustrated. If plain, the color of the cover is noted, e.g., plain blue, etc. If the cover is printed directly onto the bookcover, that is noted as "illustrated." A "DJ" in the entry indicates a dust jacket.

Series – This is the line or series under which the book was published.

Pages – This is the number of pages of text that the version of the book contains. Where the pages are unnumbered, the abbreviation "unp." is used meaning that the book is unpaged.

Value – Prices listed are for books in fine condition. Deductions must be made for books in lesser conditions. Generally, each step down in grade will mean a deduction of 25 percent from the better grade. For example, a book that lists for $10.00 in fine condition would be worth $5.00 in very good condition and $3.75 in good condition. The presence of a dust jacket in very good condition or better will usually command a premium of at least 50 percent.

Value Guide

Books by Title

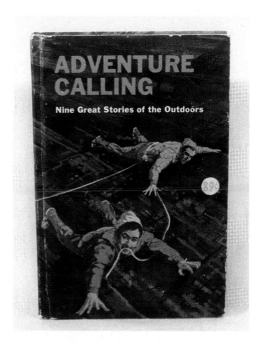

❖ADVENTURE CALLING
Nine Great Stories of the Outdoors❖
#1621; 1969; Greiner, N. Gretchen & William
H. Larson; illustrated; Whitman® Classics; 212
pgs.; $4.00

❖ADVENTURES OF
SHERLOCK HOLMES❖
#2717; 1965; Doyle, A. Conan;
illustrated; Whitman® Classics
Library; 254 pgs.; $6.00

❖ADVENTURES OF
 SHERLOCK HOLMES❖
#1612:49; 1955; Doyle, A. Conan;
illustrated; Whitman® Classics; 282
pgs.; $8.00

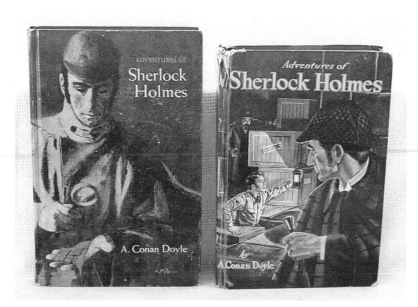

❖ADVENTURES WITH HAL❖
#1755; 1965; Bond, Gladys Baker; illus-
trated; Whitman® Tween Age Book; 156
pgs.; $5.00

❖ALICE IN WONDERLAND❖
#1616; 1970; Carroll, Lewis;
illustrated; Whitman® Classics;
212 pgs.; $5.00

❖IN THE AIR WITH ANDY LANE
15 Days in the Air❖
#2302; 1928; Adams, Eustace L.;
plain lt. green; (DJ); Whitman®
Books For Boys; 194 pgs.; $22.00

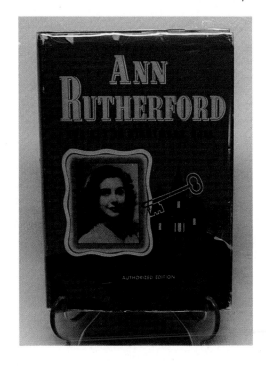

❖ANN RUTHERFORD
And The Key to Nightmare Hall❖
#2372; 1942; Heisenfelt, Kathryn;
plain green; (DJ); Whitman® Authorized Edition; 246 pgs.; $18.00

(Made her screen debut in 1935.
Appeared in *Laramie Trail*, *Secret
Life of Walter Mitty*, and *Adventures
of Don Juan*, among others.)

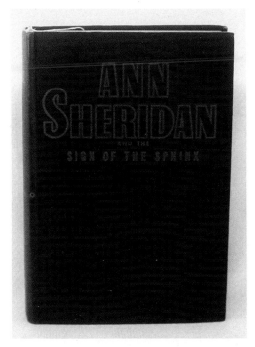

❖ANN SHERIDAN
And The Sign of the Sphinx❖ #2390; 1943;
Heisenfelt, Kathryn; plain brown; Whitman®
Authorized Edition; 248 pgs.; $20.00

(Born in Denton, Texas. First role was in
Search For Beauty in 1933. Pictures include
They Drive by Night, *I Was a Male War Bride*,
Edge of Darkness, and *Shine on Harvest
Moon*.)

❖ANNIE OAKLEY
In Danger at Diablo❖
#1540:49; 1955; Schroeder, Doris;
illustrated; Authorized TV Edition; 282
pgs.; $30.00

(81 episodes were produced from
April 1953 until December 1956. They
aired on ABC daytime and in syndication. Photo cover of Gail Davis as
Annie Oakley.)

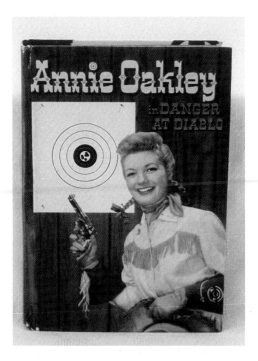

❖BARRY BLAKE
Of the Flying Fortress❖ #2394; 1943;
DuBois, Gaylord; plain blue; Fighters
For Freedom Series; 248 pgs.; $15.00

❖BASKET FEVER❖
#1537; 1970; Bowen, Robert Sidney;
illustrated; Sports Stories; 210 pgs.;
$5.00

❖BAT MASTERSON❖
#1550; 1960; Lee, Wayne C.; illustrated;
Authorized TV Adventure; 282 pgs.;
$20.00

(First aired 10/08/59 on NBC. Ran to
09/21/61. Starred Gene Barry as a
debonair gambler/lawman armed with a
cane, derby hat, and a custom-built gun.)

❖BATCH OF THE BEST, A
Stories for Girls❖
#1623; 1970; Various; illustrated;
Whitman® Classics; 211 pgs.; $4.00

❖BEAUTIFUL JOE❖
#1625; 1955; Saunders, Marshall;
illustrated; Whitman® Classics; 283
pgs.; $6.00

❖BEAUTIFUL JOE❖
#2712; 1965; Saunders, Marshall;
illustrated; Whitman® Classics; 254
pgs.; $4.00

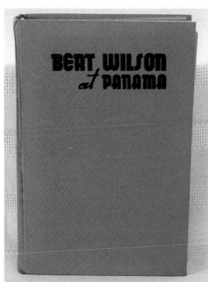

❖BERT WILSON AT PANAMA❖
#2351; 1940; Duffield, J.W.; plain
orange; Young People's Adventures;
252 pgs.; $10.00

❖BETTER MAN, THE
With Some Account of What He Struggled For
and What He Won❖
No #; 1910; Brady, Cyrus Townsend; plain blue;
186 pgs.; $8.00

❖BETTY GRABLE
And The House of Cobwebs❖
#2306; 1947; Heisenfelt, Kathryn;
plain brown; (DJ); Whitman®
Authorized Edition; 250 pgs.;
$25.00

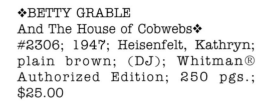

❖BETTY GRABLE
And The House with the Iron Shutters❖
#2386; 1943; Heisenfelt, Kathryn; plain
brown; (DJ); Authorized Edition; 252 pgs.;
$16.00

(Born 12/18/16, Ms. Grable first appeared in
What Price Innocence? in 1933. Band singer,
dancer, vaudevillian and actress, she is one of
the classic greats to come out of the Hollywood
dream machine.)

❖BEVERLY HILLBILLIES, THE
The Saga of Wildcat Creek❖ #1572; 1963;
Schroeder, Doris; illustrated; Authorized
TV Adventure; 212 pgs.; $20.00

(First aired 09/26/62 on CBS. Ran to
09/07/71. The hapless adventures of Jed,
Granny, Elly Mae and Jethro played by
Buddy Ebsen, Irene Ryan, Donna Douglas
and Max Baer, respectively. Jumped to
the top of the ratings. Paul Henning, the
show's writer, also worked on *The Real
McCoys*.)

❖BEWITCHED,
The Opposite Uncle❖
#1572; 1970; Johnston, William; illustrated; Authorized
TV Edition; 212 pgs.; $35.00

(First aired on 09/17/64 on ABC. Ran to 07/01/72.
Starred Elizabeth Montgomery, Dick Sargent, Agnes More-
head and twins Erin and Diane Murphy as Samantha, Darrin, Endora and Tabitha, respectively. Montgomery
starred as a beautiful young witch trying to give up witch-
craft in order to please her dullard husband. Her mother
continually interferred with their relationship. Dick York
originally played Darrin but had to leave in 1969 because
of a back injury. The show's ratings dropped and never
recovered.)

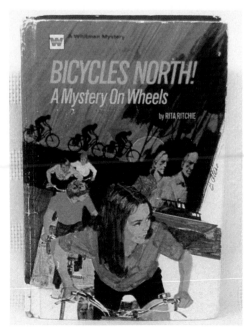

❖BICYCLES NORTH
A Mystery On Wheels❖
#1571; 1973; Ritchie, Rita; illustrated;
Whitman® Mystery; 210 pgs.; $4.00

❖BIG VALLEY, THE❖
#1569; 1966; Hecklemann, Charles; illustrated; Authorized TV Edition; 214 pgs.; $25.00

(First aired 09/15/65 on ABC. Ran to 05/19/69. Starred Barbara Stanwyck, Richard Long, Peter Breck, Lee Majors, and Linda Evans as Victoria, Jarrod, Nick, Heath, and Audra Barkley. Served as Lee Majors' first acting role.)

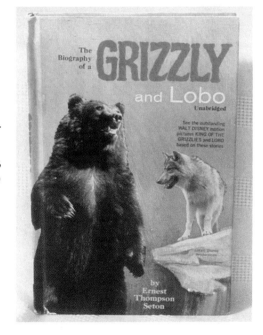

❖BIOGRAPHY OF A GRIZZLY AND LOBO, THE❖
#1622; 1969; Seton, Ernest Thompson; illustrated; Whitman® Classics; 138 pgs.; $8.00

❖BLACK BEAUTY❖
#1604; 1955; Sewell, Anna; illustrated; Whitman® Classics; 284 pgs.; $8.00

(Two variations of the cover shown.)

❖BLONDIE
And Dagwood's Adventure In Magic❖
#2300; 1944; Young, Chic; plain lt. green;
(DJ); Young People Fiction; 248 pgs.; $18.00

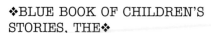

❖BLONDIE
And Dagwood's Snapshot Clue❖
#2388; 1943; Young, Chic; plain brown; Authorized
Edition; 247 pgs.; $12.00

(Blondie first appeared in the *New York American*
on 9/15/30. It was conceived as the story of a gold
digger flapper pursuing a naive playboy.)

❖BLUE BOOK OF CHILDREN'S
STORIES, THE❖
#4059; 1934; Various; illustrated; Whit-
man® Classics; unp.; $13.00

❖BLUE STREAK And Doctor Medusa❖
#2313; 1946; Elder, Art; plain brown; Authorized Edition; 248 pgs.; $14.00

(Comic book character which first appeared in Holyoke One-Shot #4 in 1944.)

❖BLYTHE GIRLS, THE
Helen, Margy and Rose❖
#2320; 1925; Hope, Laura Lee; plain red; Adventures For Girls; 214 pgs.; $8.00

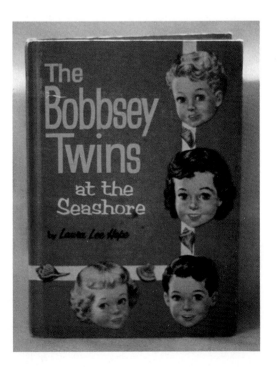

❖BOBBSEY TWINS, THE
At the Seashore❖
#2332; 1954; Hope, Laura Lee; illustrated; Bobbsey Twins Series; 282 pgs.; $6.00

❖BOBBSEY TWINS, THE
In the Country❖
#1530; 1953; Hope, Laura Lee;
illustrated; Bobbsey Twins Series;
282 pgs.; $6.00

❖BOBBSEY TWINS, THE
Merry Days Indoors and Out❖
#2342; 1950; Hope, Laura Lee; (DJ); Bobbsey
Twins Series; 216 pgs.; $12.00

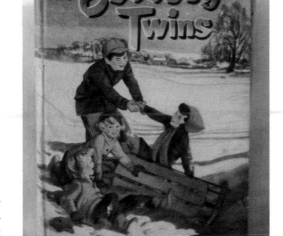

❖BOBBSEY TWINS, THE
Merry Days Indoors and Out❖
#1531; 1950; Hope, Laura Lee; illus-
trated; Bobbsey Twins Series; 282
pgs.; $6.00

❖BOBBY BLAKE
At Bass Cove or The Hunt
for the Motor Boat Gem❖
#2301; 1915; Warner, Frank A.; plain tan;
Boys Adventures; 254 pgs.; $10.00

❖BOBBY BLAKE
At Rockledge School❖
#2300; 1915; Warner, Frank A.;
plain lt. red; (DJ); Boys Adventures;
256 pgs.; $12.00

❖BONANZA
Killer Lion❖
#1568; 1966; Frazee, Steve; illustrated; Authorized
TV Adventure; 212 pgs.; $18.00

(First aired 09/12/59 on NBC. Ran to 01/16/73.
Starred Lorne Greene, Dan Blocker (until '72),
Michael Landon and Pernell Roberts (until '65). The
highest rated show for many years. The first western to be televised in color.)

❖BONITA GRANVILLE
And The Mystery of Star Island❖
#2371; 1942; Heisenfelt, Kathryn; plain green; (DJ); Whitman® Authorized Edition; 248 pgs.; $12.00

(Ms. Granville appeared in one of the great sleepers of movie history, *Hitler's Children* in 1943. This movie received the first all-out radio promotion campaign ever mounted.)

❖BOOTS
And The Mystery of the Unlucky Vase❖
#2387; 1943; Martin, Edgar; plain blue; (DJ); Whitman® Authorized Edition; 248 pgs.; $25.00

(*Boots and Her Buddies* was a comic strip penned by Edgar Martin. Launched in 1924, she was the most frankly glamorous of the funny females in the '20s. Over the next 20 years she grew from a college girl to a flapper, a modern woman, a wife and a mother.)

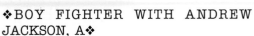

❖BOY FIGHTER WITH ANDREW JACKSON, A❖
#2331; 1946; Thomas, H.C.; Plain Brown; Whitman® Authorized Edition; 249 pgs.; $20.00

(This copy is an error. The book is mounted in the cover backwards. Value with normal binding, $8.00.)

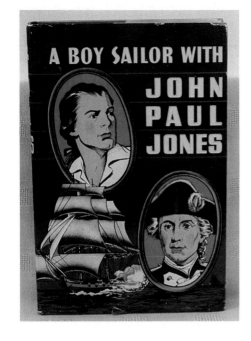

❖BOY SAILOR WITH
JOHN PAUL JONES, A❖
#2314; 1946; Thomas, H.C.; plain
tan; (DJ); Authorized Edition; 250
pgs.; $8.00

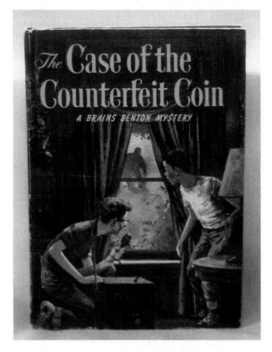

❖BRAINS BENTON
The Case of the Counterfeit Coin❖
#1561; 1960; Wyatt, George; illustrated;
Whitman® Mystery; 188 pgs.; $6.00

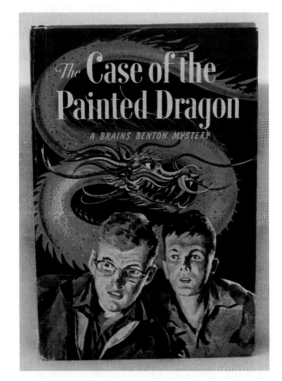

❖BRAINS BENTON
The Case of the Painted Dragon❖
#1565; 1961; Wyatt, George; illus-
trated; Brains Benton Mystery;
185 pgs.; $5.00

❖BRAINS BENTON
The Case of the Roving Rolls❖
#1563; 1961; Wyatt, George; illustrated;
Brains Benton Mystery Series; 186 pgs.;
$5.00

❖BRAINS BENTON
The Case of the Stolen Dummy❖
#1562; 1961; Wyatt, George; illustrated;
Brains Benton Mystery; 186 pgs.; $5.00

❖BRENDA STARR
Girl Reporter❖
#2383; 1943; Messick, Dale; plain
brown; (DJ); Whitman® Authorized Edition; 248 pgs.; $30.00

(Brenda Starr first appeared in 1940 in
the *Tribune-News* Syndicate.)

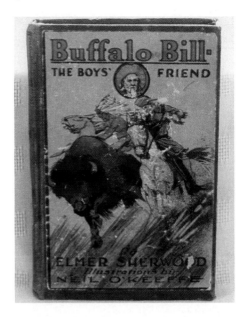

❖BUFFALO BILL
The Boys' Friend❖
No #; 1917; Sherwood, Elmer; illustrated
paper; Boy's Adventure; 246 pgs.; $15.00

❖CALL OF THE WILD, THE❖
#1635; 1970; London, Jack;
illustrated; Whitman® Classics;
210 pgs.; $4.00

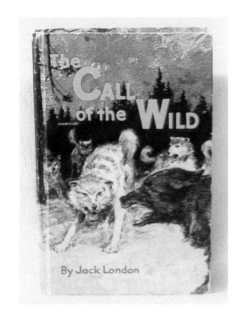

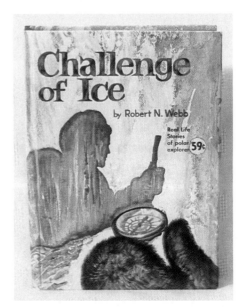

❖CHALLENGE OF ICE
Real Life Stories of Polar Explorers❖
#1506; 1963; Webb, Robert N.; illustrat-
ed; Real Life Stories; 212 pgs.; $6.00

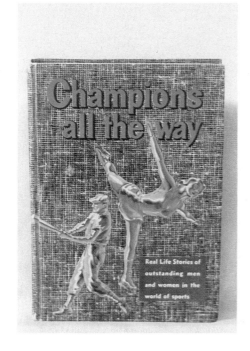

❖CHAMPIONS ALL THE WAY
Real Life Stories of Outstanding Men
and Women in the World of Sports❖
#1514; 1960; Meyers, Barlow; illus-
trated; Real Life Stories; 210 pgs.;
$6.00

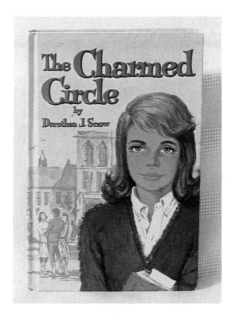

❖CHARMED CIRCLE, THE❖
#1555; 1962; Snow, Dorothea J.; illustrated;
Whitman® Novel For Girls; 216 pgs.; $5.00

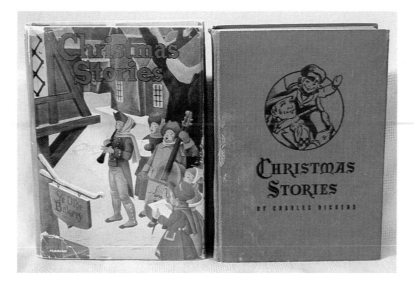

❖CHRISTMAS STORIES❖
#2144; 1951; Various; plain block;
(DJ); Whitman Classics; 235 pgs.;
$8.00
❖CHRISTMAS STORIES
A Christmas Carol and Others❖
No #; 1940; Dickens, Charles;
plain blue; Whitman® Classics;
235 pgs.; $10.00

❖CIRCUS BOY Under the Big Top❖
#1549; 1957; Snow, Dorothea J.; illustrated; Authorized TV Edition; 282 pgs.; $25.00

(First aired on NBC on 09/23/56 until 09/57 when it was picked up by ABC. It ran there till 09/11/58. Reruns continued on Saturday mornings until 09/60. Starred Mickey Braddock (Dolenz) as Corky, Noah Beery, Jr. as Joey the Clown and Billy Barty as Little Tom.)

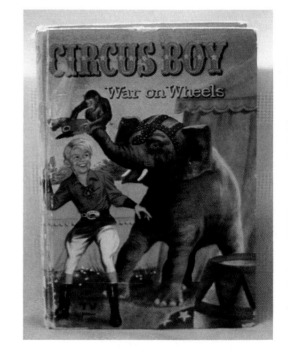

❖CIRCUS BOY War On Wheels❖
#1578; 1958; Snow, Dorothea J.; illustrated; Authorized TV Edition; 282 pgs.; $25.00

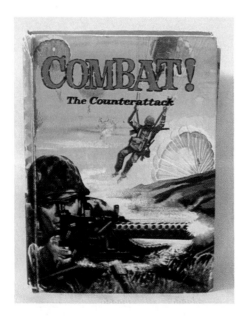

❖COMBAT
The Counterattack❖
#1520; 1964; Davis, Franklin M. Jr.; illustrated; Authorized TV Adventure; 210 pgs.; $20.00

(First aired 10/02/62 on ABC. Ran to 08/29/67. Starred Rick Jason and Vic Morrow as Lt. Gil Hanley and Sgt. Chip Saunders. War drama set in post-D-day Europe. Directed by Robert Altman.)

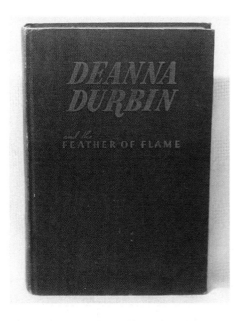

❖DEANNA DURBIN
And The Feather of Flame❖
#2356; 1941; Heisenfelt, Kathryn; plain green;
Authorized Edition; 220 pgs.; $10.00

(In 1937, at age 15, Miss Durbin's pure soprano
captured the nation's interest in "One Hundred
Men and A Girl." The men were Leopold Stokowski
and his symphonic orchestra.)

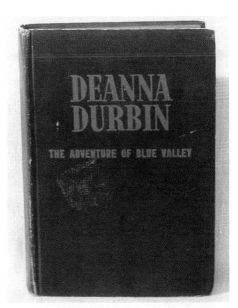

❖DEANNA DURBIN
The Adventure of Blue Valley❖
#2355; 1941; Heisenfelt, Kathryn; plain
brown; Authorized Edition; 220 pgs.;
$10.00

❖DEFIANT HEART, THE❖
#2310; 1964; Michelson, Florence
B.; illustrated; Whitman® Teen
Novel; 288 pgs.; $5.00

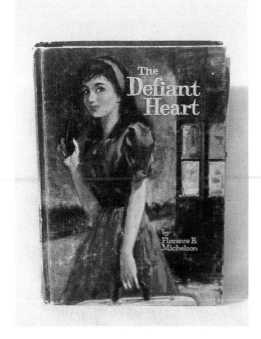

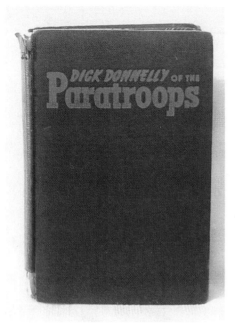

❖DICK DONNELLY
of the Paratroops❖
#2307; 1944; Duncan, Gregory; plain green;
Fighters For Freedom Series; 248 pgs.; $13.00

❖DICK TRACY Ace Detective❖
#2381; 1943; Gould, Chester; plain
brown; Comic Strip; 248 pgs.; $20.00

(This character was created by Chester
Gould and first appeared on 09/01/31.
Gould originally named the strip "Plain-
clothes Tracy" but his publisher
changed the name to its present form.)

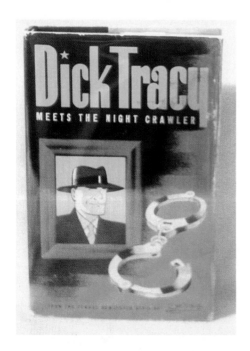

❖DICK TRACY Meets the Night Crawler❖
#2310; 1945; Gould, Chester; plain blue; (DJ);
Whitman® Authorized Edition; 247 pgs.;
$25.00

❖DIVERS DOWN Adventure Under Hawaiian Seas❖
#1554; 1971; Gordon, Hal; illustrated; Sports and
Adventure Stories; 210 pgs.; $5.00

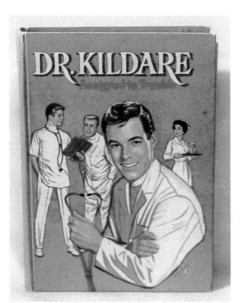

❖DR. KILDARE
Assigned To Trouble❖
#1547; 1963; Ackworth, Robert C.; illustrated;
Authorized TV Adventure; 212 pgs.; $12.00

(First aired 09/28/61 on NBC. Ran to
08/30/66. Starred Richard Chamberlain and
Raymond Massey as Dr. James Kildare and Dr.
Leonard Gillespie. The first of the medical
drama genre. Based on a series of books written by Max Brand in the '30s.)

❖DR. KILDARE
The Magic Key❖
#1519; 1964; Johnston, William; illus-
trated; Authorized TV Edition; 210
pgs.; $10.00

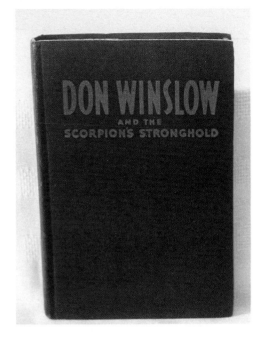

❖DON WINSLOW
And the Scorpion's Stronghold❖
#2327; 1946; Martinek, Frank V.; plain green;
Authorized Edition; 248 pgs.; $12.00

(Began as "Winslow of the Navy," a Bell Syndicate comic strip in 1934. Also was adapted to
radio as a children's serial program around
1938. Lt. Cmdr. Martinek was Fleet Intelligence
Officer to the Asiatic Fleet and organized the
Physical, Chemical, and Photographic Lab for
Naval Intelligence.)

❖DONNA PARKER
A Spring To Remember❖
#1594; 1960; Martin, Marcia; illus-
trated; Whitman® Adventure; 282
pgs.; $8.00

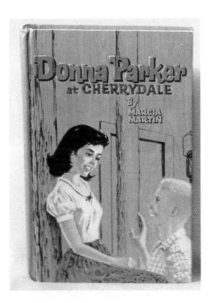

❖DONNA PARKER
At Cherrydale❖
#1590; 1957; Martin, Marcia; illustrated;
Whitman® Adventure; 282 pgs.; $8.00

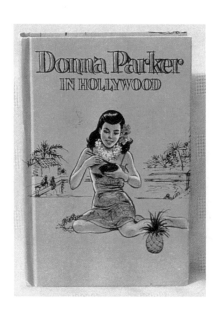

❖DONNA PARKER
In Hollywood❖
#1593; 1956; Martin, Marcia; illustrated; Whitman® Adventure; 282 pgs.; $10.00

❖DONNA PARKER
Mystery at Arawak❖
#1540; 1962; Martin, Marcia; illustrated; Mysteries For Girls; 282 pgs.; $8.00

❖DONNA PARKER
On Her Own❖
#1592; 1957; Martin, Marcia; illustrated; Whitman® Adventure; 282 pgs.; $8.00

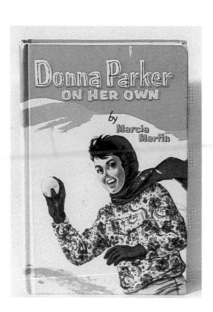

❖DONNA PARKER
Special Agent❖
#1591; 1957; Martin, Marcia; illus-
trated; Whitman® Adventure; 282
pgs.; $8.00

❖DONNA PARKER
Takes A Giant Step❖
#1589; 1954; Martin, Marcia; illustrat-
ed; Whitman® Adventure; 282 pgs.;
$8.00

❖DORY BOY❖
#1760; 1966; Weiss, Joan Talmage; illustrat-
ed; Whitman® Tween Age Book; 156 pgs.;
$5.00

❖DRAG STRIP DANGER❖
#1503; 1972; Olney, Ross R.; illustrated;
Whitman® Novel; 212 pgs.; $5.00

❖DRAGNET
Case Stories❖
#1527; 1957; Deming, Richard; illustrated;
Authorized TV Edition; 282 pgs.; $25.00

(First aired 01/03/52 on NBC. Ran to
09/10/70. Starred Jack Webb and Ben Alexander as Sgt. Joe Friday and Officer Frank Smith.
Henry Morgan joined the cast in 1967. Police
drama highlighted the deductive process used to
solve actual cases.)

❖EIGHT COUSINS❖
#1618; 1955; Alcott, Louisa May;
illustrated; Whitman® Classics; 284
pgs.; $4.00

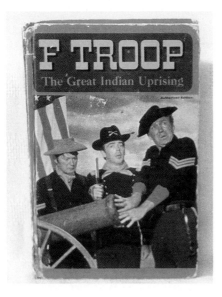

❖F TROOP The Great Indian Uprising❖
#1544; 1967; Johnston, William; illustrated;
Authorized TV Edition; 214 pgs.; $25.00

(First aired 09/14/65 on ABC. Ran to
08/31/67. Starred Ken Berry, Forrest Tucker,
Larry Storch and Melody Patterson as Capt.
William Parmenter, Sgt. Morgan O'Rourke, Cpl.
Randolph Agarn and Wrangler Jane.)

❖FAMILY AFFAIR
Buffy Finds a Star❖
#1567; 1970; Bond, Gladys Baker;
illustrated; Authorized TV Edition; 140
pgs.; $15.00

(Ex-Lib. First aired 09/12/66 on CBS.
Ran to 09/09/71. Starred Brian Keith,
Sebastian Cabot, Anissa Jones and
Johnnie Whittaker as Bill Davis, Mr.
Giles French, Buffy and Jody.)

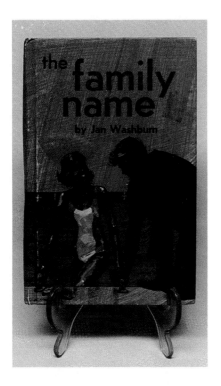

❖FAMILY NAME, THE❖
#1531; 1971; Washburn, Jan; illustrated;
Whitman® Novels For Girls; 210 pgs.; $8.00

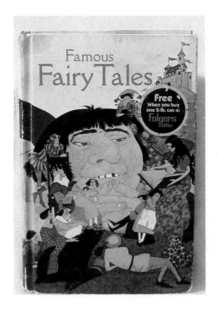

❖FAMOUS FAIRY TALES❖
#1609; 1971; Various; illustrated; Whitman® Classics; 210 pgs.; $15.00

(This book was a promotional giveaway. It was free with the purchase of a 2-pound can of Folgers Coffee.)

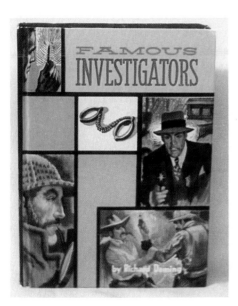

❖FAMOUS INVESTIGATORS❖
#1564; 1963; Deming, Richard; illustrated; Real Life Stories; 210 pgs.; $6.00

❖FAVORITE STORIES
A Collection of the Best-Loved Tales of Childhood❖
#2106; 1968; Various; illustrated; Whitman® Giant Book; 223 pgs.; $10.00

❖FIFTY FAMOUS AMERICANS❖
#2129; 1946; Griffith, Ward; plain brown; (DJ);
Whitman® Classics; 236 pgs.; $15.00

❖FIVE LITTLE PEPPERS
And How They Grew❖
#1609:49; 1955; Sidney, Margaret; illus-
trated; Fiction For Young People; 284
pgs.; $6.00

❖FIVE LITTLE PEPPERS❖
And How They Grew❖
#1609; 1955; Sidney, Margaret; illus-
trated; Whitman® Classics; 284 pgs.;
$4.00

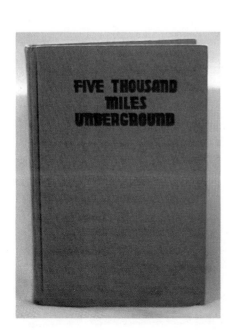

❖FIVE THOUSAND MILES UNDERGROUND❖
#2345; 1913; Rockwood, Roy; plain red;
Great Marvel Series; 242 pgs.; $12.00

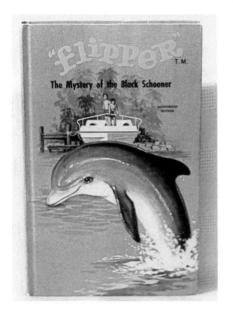

❖"FLIPPER"
The Mystery of the Black Schooner❖
#2324; 1966; Hardwick, Richard; illustrated;
Authorized TV Adventure; 190 pgs.; $15.00

(First aired 09/19/64 on NBC. Ran to 09/01/68.
Starred Suzy, Brian Kelly and Tommy Norden as
Flipper, Porter Ricks and Bud Ricks. An adventure
based in Coral Keys Park in Florida.)

❖FRECKLES❖
#1613; 1961; Porter, Gene Stratton; illustrated;
Whitman® Classics; 284 pgs.; $4.00

❖FRECKLES❖
#2713; 1961; Porter, Gene Stratton;
illustrated; Whitman® Classics; 284
pgs.; $5.00

❖FURY
And The Lone Pine Mystery❖
#1537; 1957; Fenton, William; illustrated;
Authorized TV Edition; 282 pgs.; $25.00

(Saturday morning show starring Bobby Diamond, Gypsy, and Peter Graves. Sponsored by
Post Cereals on NBC.)

❖ FURY
And The Mystery at Trapper's Hole❖
#1557; 1959; Nesbit, Troy; illustrated;
Authorized TV Edition; 282 pgs.; $18.00

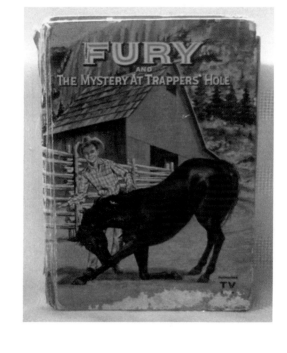

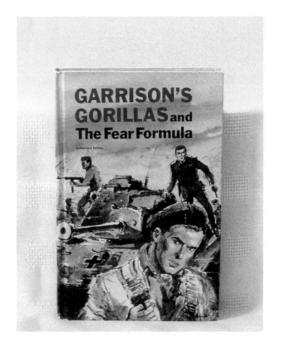

❖GARRISON'S GORILLAS
And The Fear Formula❖
#1548; 1968; Pearl, Jack; illustrated; Autho-
rized TV Adventure; 210 pgs.; $20.00

(First aired 09/05/67 on ABC. Ran to 09/17/68.
Starred Ron Harper as Lt. Craig Garrison. War
drama featuring convicts recruited to fight the
Nazis with the promise of a pardon.)

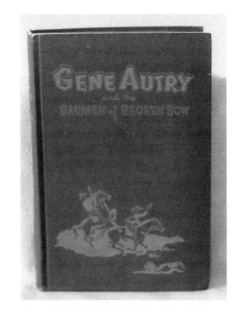

❖GENE AUTRY
And The Badmen of Broken Bow❖
#2355; 1951; Miller, Snowden; plain sienna;
Whitman® Authorized Edition; 250 pgs.; $15.00

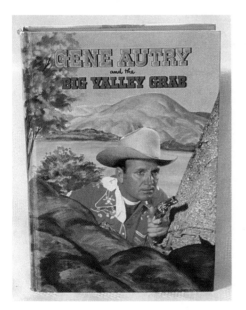

❖GENE AUTRY
And The Big Valley Grab❖
#2302:49; 1954; Hutchinson, W.H.; illustrated;
Whitman® Authorized Edition; 282 pgs.;
$25.00

❖GENE AUTRY
And The Ghost Riders❖
#1510:49; 1955; Patten, Lewis B.;
illustrated; Whitman® Authorized Edition; 282 pgs.; $20.00

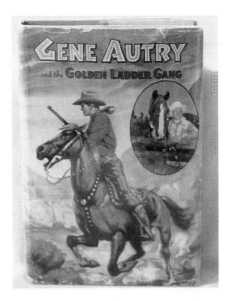

❖GENE AUTRY
And The Golden Ladder Gang❖
#2349; 1950; Hutchinson, W.H.; plain tan; (DJ);
Whitman® Authorized Edition; 250 pgs.; $25.00

(Autry's screen debut was in 1934 at Mascot
Pictures, later to become Republic, as the
screen's first singing cowboy. Autry was a
1930s radio singer who brought rural audiences
back to the screen.)

❖GENE AUTRY
And The Golden Stallion❖
#1511:49; 1954; Fannin, Cole; illustrat-
ed; Whitman® Authorized Edition; 282
pgs.; $20.00

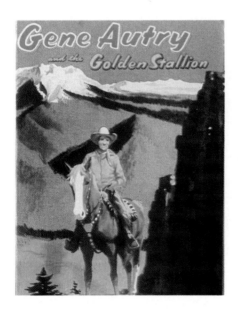

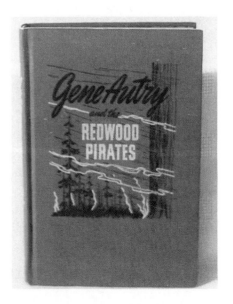

❖GENE AUTRY And The Redwood Pirates❖
#2326; 1946; Hamilton, Bob; plain tan; Whit-
man® Authorized Edition; 248 pgs.; $12.00

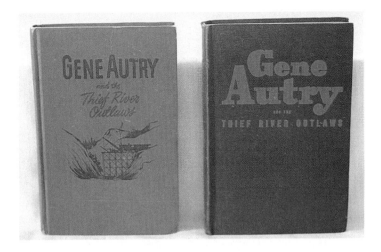

❖GENE AUTRY
And The Thief River Outlaws❖
#2303; 1944; Hamilton, Bob; plain
orange or plain brown; Fiction For Boys;
249 pgs.; $14.00

❖GILLIGAN'S ISLAND❖
#1566; 1966; Johnston, William; illustrated;
Authorized TV Edition; 212 pgs.; $30.00

(First aired on CBS on 09/26/64. Ran to
09/04/67. Starred Bob Denver as Willie Gilligan,
Alan Hale, Jr. as Jonas Grumby, Jim Backus as
Thurston Howell III, Natalie Schafer as Lovey Howell, Tina Louise as Ginger Grant, Russell Johnson
as Roy Hinkley, and Dawn Wells as Mary Ann
Summers.)

❖GINGER ROGERS And The Riddle
of the Scarlet Cloak❖
#2378; 1942; Rogers, Lela E.; plain
brown; (DJ); Whitman® Authorized
Edition; 248 pgs.; $25.00

(The prettier half of the Rogers/
Astaire dance duo.)

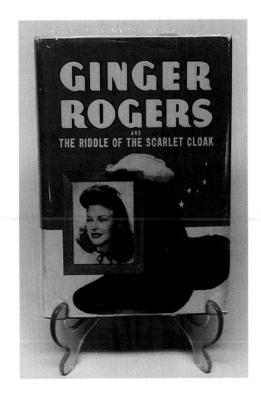

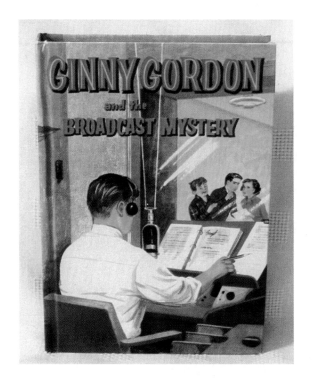

❖GINNY GORDON
And The Broadcast Mystery❖
#1554:49; 1956; Campbell, Julie; illustrated;
Fiction for Young People; 282 pgs.; $8.00

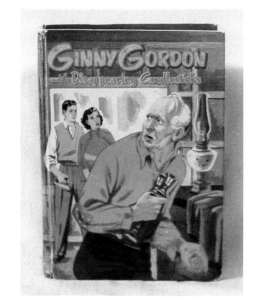

❖GINNY GORDON And The Disappearing Candlesticks❖
#1575; 1954; Campbell, Julie;
illustrated; Whitman® Mystery;
282 pgs.; $8.00

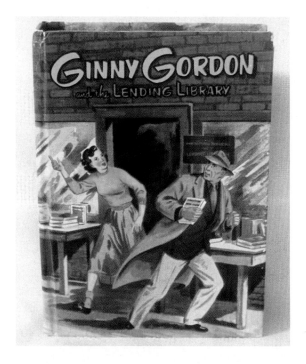

❖GINNY GORDON
And The Lending Library❖
#1523; 1971; Campbell, Julie; illustrated;
Whitman® Mystery; 282 pgs.; $8.00

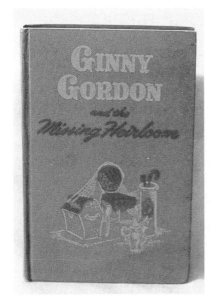

❖GINNY GORDON
And The Missing Heirloom❖
#2352; 1950; Campbell, Julie; plain
green; Whitman® Mystery; 249 pgs.;
$10.00

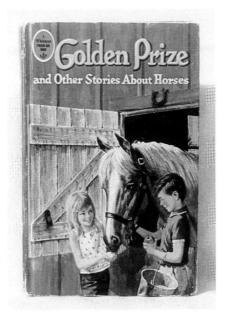

❖GOLDEN PRIZE
And Other Stories About Horses❖
#1753; 1965; Various; illustrated; Whit-
man® Tween Age Book; 156 pgs.; $6.00

❖GREAT WAR, THE
Stories of World War I❖
#1579; 1965; Jablonski, Edward;
illustrated; Real Life Stories; 210 pgs.;
$6.00

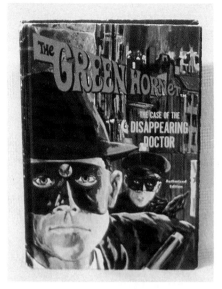

❖GREEN HORNET, THE
The Case of the Disappearing Doctor❖
#1570; 1966; Keith, Brandon; illustrated; Authorized TV Edition; 212 pgs.; $35.00

(First aired 09/09/66 on ABC. Ran to 07/14/67. Starred Van Williams and Bruce Lee as Britt Reid, The Green Hornet and Kato. Crime drama based on media magnate Reid's masked alter ego.)

❖GUNSMOKE
Showdown On Front Street❖
#1520; 1969; Newman, Paul S.; illustrated; Authorized TV Adventure; 210 pgs.; $15.00

(First aired 09/10/55 on CBS. Ran to 09/01/75. Expanded to one hour in 1961. Started as a radio program in 1952. Three months after it started, the release of the film *High Noon* convinced executives that the American viewing public was ready for a western format.)

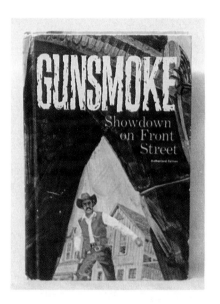

❖GYPSY FROM NOWHERE❖
#1509; 1972; Wagner, Sharon; illustrated; Whitman® Adventure; 210 pgs.; $6.00

❖HAL KEEN
Hermit of Gordon's Creek❖
#2312; 1931; Lloyd, Hugh; plain tan; Whitman® Mystery; 237 pgs.; $6.00

❖HAVE GUN, WILL TRAVEL❖
#1568; 1959; Meyers, Barlow; illustrated; Authorized TV Edition; 282 pgs.; $25.00

(First aired 09/14/57 on CBS. Ran to 09/21/63. Starred Richard Boone as Paladin. Western featuring an educated, refined, disciplined and deadly gun for hire.)

❖HAWAII FIVE-O
The Octopus Caper❖
#1553; 1971; Ellis, Leo R.; illustrated; Authorized TV Adventure; 212 pgs.; $18.00

(First aired on CBS 09/26/68 through 04/26/80. Starred Jack Lord as Detective Steve McGarrett. Police drama based on the Five-O group which was attached to the state police.)

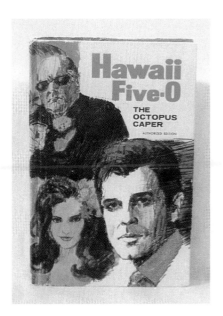

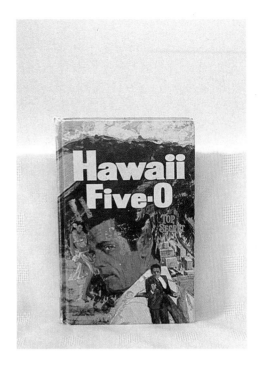

❖HAWAII FIVE-O
Top Secret❖
#1511; 1969; Bowen, Robert Sidney; illustrated; Authorized TV Adventure; 210 pgs.; $15.00

(First aired 09/26/68 on CBS. Ran to 04/26/80. Starred Jack Lord and James MacArthur as Det. Steve McGarrett and Danny "Danno" Williams. A scenery-driven engine intended to sidestep gun shy sentiments in the wake of the King/Kennedy assassinations.)

❖HEIDI❖
#2121; 1944; Spyri, Johanna; block print; Whitman® Classics; 234 pgs.; $4.00

❖HEIDI
Grows Up❖
1608; 1971; Tritten, Charles; illustrated; Whitman® Classics; 210 pgs.; $4.00

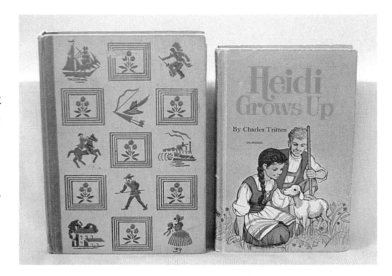

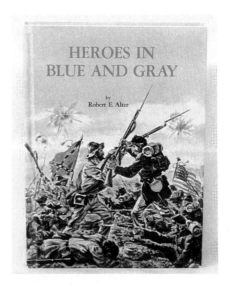

❖HEROES IN BLUE AND GRAY❖
#1580; 1965; Alter, Robert E.; illustrated; Real Life Stories; 212 pgs.; $6.00

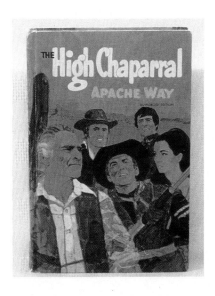

❖HIGH CHAPARRAL
The Apache Way❖
#1519; 1969; Frazee, Steve; illustrated; Authorized TV Edition; 210 pgs.; $15.00

(First aired on NBC 09/10/67. Ran through 09/10/71. Starred Leif Erickson as Big John Cannon and Cameron Mitchell as Buck Cannon. Western highlighting the struggle to establish a cattle empire.)

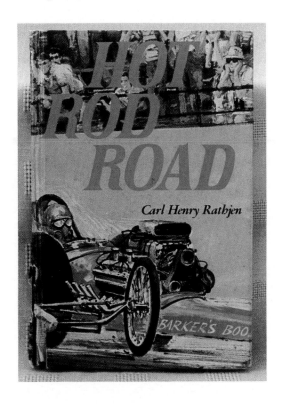

❖HOT ROD ROAD❖
#1582; 1968; Rathjen, Carl Henry; illustrated; Sports Stories; 210 pgs.; $6.00

❖HUCKLEBERRY FINN❖
#1606; 1955; Twain, Mark; illustrated; Whitman® Classics; 284 pgs.; $8.00

❖HUCKLEBERRY FINN❖
#2719; 1965; Twain, Mark; illustrated; Whitman® Classics; 254 pgs.; $5.00

❖I SPY
Message From Moscow❖
#1542; 1966; Keith, Brandon; illustrated;
Authorized TV Edition; 210 pgs.; $25.00

(First aired on NBC on 09/15/65. Ran through
09/02/68. Starred Robert Culp as Kelly Robinson and Bill Cosby as Alexander Scott. Cosby
was the first black performer to star in a serious drama.)

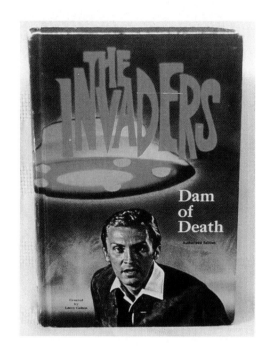

❖INVADERS, THE
Dam of Death❖
#1545; 1967; Pearl, Jack; illustrated;
Authorized TV Adventure; 212 pgs.; $15.00

(Ran from 01/10/67 to 09/17/68 on ABC.
Starred Roy Thinnes as David Vincent. A science fiction drama based on the idea that
aliens are already on Earth, scouting for a
much larger invasion force.)

❖INVISIBLE SCARLET O'NEIL❖
#2382; 1943; Stamm, Russell; plain brown;
(DJ); Whitman® Authorized Edition; 248 pgs.;
$28.00

(Based on a comic book story started in
Famous Funnies #81 in 1939. The story ended
in Famous Funnies #167 published by Eastern
Color. Reappeared in 1950 under the Famous
Funnies label by Harvey. Final appearance in
1952 in Harvey Comics Hits #59.)

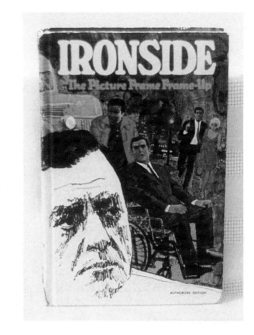

❖IRONSIDE
The Picture Frame Frame-Up❖
#1521; 1969; Johnston, William; illustrated;
Authorized TV Adventure; 212 pgs.; $15.00

(First aired on NBC on 09/14/67. Ran to
01/16/75. Starred Raymond Burr as a wheelchair-
bound special consultant to the San Francisco
Police Department.)

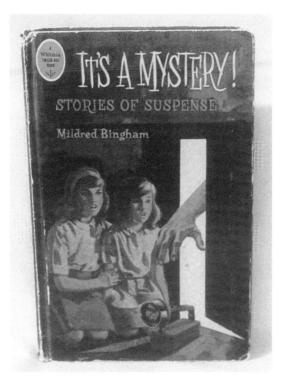

❖IT'S A MYSTERY!
Stories of Suspense❖
#1757; 1965; Bingham, Mildred; illustrated;
Whitman® Tween Age Book; 156 pgs.; $6.00

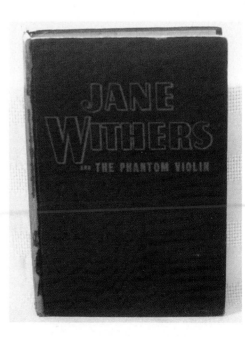

❖JANE WITHERS
And The Phantom Violin❖
#2389; 1943; Snell, Roy J.; plain green;
Authorized Edition; 248 pgs.; $14.00

(Jane Withers appeared in *Pepper* in
1936, a 20th Century Fox release. She
played Shirley Temple's selfish friend in
Bright Eyes. Later known as Josephine the
Plumber.)

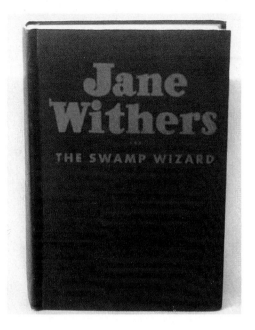

❖JANE WITHERS
And The Swamp Wizard❖
#2301; 1944; Heisenfelt, Kathryn; plain blue;
Authorized Edition; 248 pgs.; $12.00

❖JANET LENNON
Adventure at Two Rivers❖
#1536; 1961; Meyers, Barlow; illustrat-
ed; Authorized TV Adventure; 210 pgs.;
$12.00

❖JANET LENNON
And The Angels❖
#1583; 1963; Meyers, Barlow; illustrated;
Authorized TV Edition; 212 pgs.; $15.00

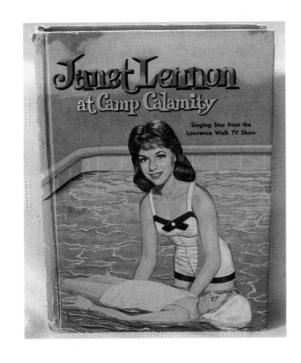

❖JANET LENNON
At Camp Calamity❖
#1539; 1962; Meyer, Barlow; illustrated;
Authorized TV Edition; 212 pgs.; $15.00

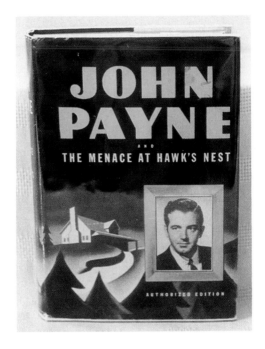

❖JOHN PAYNE
And The Menace at Hawk's Nest❖
#2385; 1943; Heisenfelt, Kathryn; plain green;
(DJ); Authorized Edition; 248 pgs.; $22.00

(John Payne lived from 1912 to 1989. Best
known for the lead in *Miracle on 34th Street*.
Married to Gloria DeHaven.)

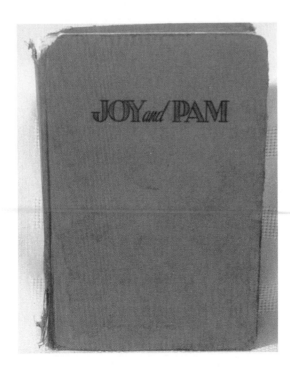

❖JOY AND PAM❖
#2358; 1927; Whitehill, Dorothy;
plain orange; Girl's Fiction; 220 pgs.;
$17.00

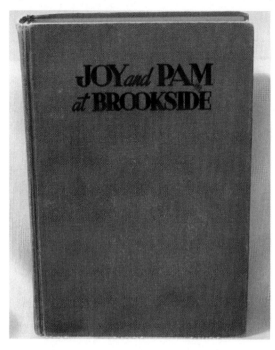

❖JOY AND PAM
At Brookside❖
#2360; 1929; Whitehill, Dorothy; plain blue;
Whitman® Girl's Fiction; 216 pgs.; $15.00

❖JOYCE OF THE SECRET SQUADRON❖
A Captain Midnight Adventure; #2376; 1942; Winterbotham, R.R.; plain green; (DJ); Authorized Edition; 251
pgs.; $25.00

(Comic book character which appeared in The Funnies
#57 by Dell Publishing. A popular, long-running radio
show and a movie serial followed. Ovaltine owns Capt.
Midnight so the syndicated TV show was called Jet Jackson, Flying Commando, but it was actually another name
for Capt. Midnight.)

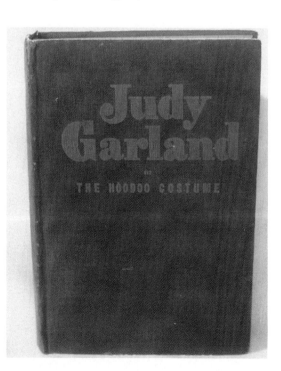

❖JUDY GARLAND
And The Hoodoo Costume❖
#2308; 1945; Heisenfelt, Kathryn; plain
brown; Whitman® Authorized Edition; 248
pgs.; $15.00

(Born Judy Gumm in Grand Rapids, Michigan,
Garland began her career in 1936 in *Pigskin
Parade*. Voted one of the 10 best money—making stars by the Herald-Fame poll in '40,'41,
and '45. Best known as Dorothy in *Wizard of
Oz*. Other notable films were *Easter Parade*
and *Meet Me In St. Louis*.)

❖JUDY JORDAN'S DISCOVERY❖
#2362; 1931; Garis, Lilian; plain
brown; Books For Girls; 248 pgs.;
$8.00

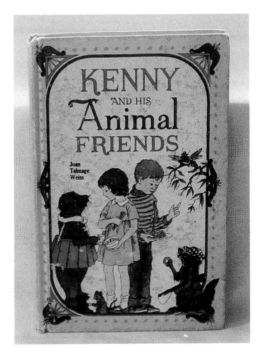

❖KENNY AND HIS ANIMAL FRIENDS❖
#1754; 1965; Weiss, Joan Talmage; illustrated;
Whitman® Tween Age Book; 156 pgs.; $10.00

❖KIDNAPPED❖
#554; 1935; Stevenson, Robert Louis;
illustrated; Whitman® Classics; 240
pgs.; $15.00

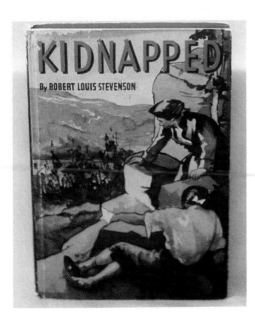

❖KIM ALDRICH MYSTERY, A
Miscalculated Risk❖
#1595; 1972; McDonnell, Jinny; illustrated;
Kim Aldrich Mystery; 211 pgs.; $4.00

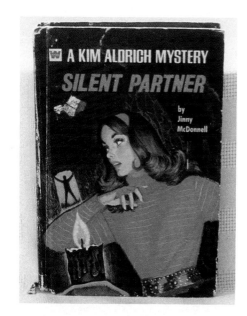

❖KIM ALDRICH MYSTERY, A;
Silent Partner❖
#1596; 1972; McDonnell, Jinny; illus-
trated; Whitman® Mystery; 210 pgs.;
$4.00

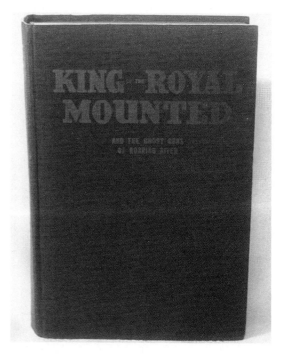

❖KING OF THE ROYAL MOUNTED
And The Ghost Guns of Roaring River❖
#2320; 1946; Grey, Zane; plain blue; Whit-
man Authorized Edition; 248 pgs.; $15.00

(King first appeared in the *American's* color
sections in 1935. Drawn by Jim Gary and
written by Zane Grey. An action hero along
the lines of the Lone Ranger.)

❖KITTY CARTER Canteen Girl❖
#2305; 1944; Radford, Ruby Lor-
raine; plain dk. green; (DJ); Fighters
For Freedom Series; 248 pgs.; $24.00

❖LAND OF THE GIANTS
Flight of Fear❖
#1516; 1969; Rathjen, Carl Henry; illustrated;
Authorized TV Adventure; 212 pgs.; $30.00

(First aired on ABC on 09/22/68. Ran to
09/06/70. Starred Gary Conway and Don Math-
eson. Science fiction drama about a group of
travelers caught up in a space warp that
deposited them on a world peopled by giants.)

❖LASSIE
And The Mystery at Blackberry Bog ❖
#1536; 1956; Snow, Dorothea J.; illustrated;
Authorized TV Adventure; 282 pgs.; $14.00

(Ran on CBS from 09/12/54 to 09/12/71. Spon-
soned by Campbell Soup. Remained in Sunday
7:00 p.m. slot through 1966. Went through several cast changes, both human and animal. The
most memorable cast was with Jon Provost as
Timmy and June Lockhart as his mother. Lassie
was derived from the 1940 novel by Eric
Knight, *Lassie Come Home*, which also inspired
MGM movie of same title.)

❖LASSIE
And The Secret of Summer❖
#1500; 1958; Snow, Dorothea J.;
illustrated; Authorized TV Adventure; 282 pgs.; $12.00

❖LASSIE
Forbidden Valley❖
#1508; 1959; Schroeder, Doris; illustrated;
Authorized TV Adventure; 282 pgs.; $18.00

❖LASSIE
Lost in the Snow❖
#1504; 1969; Frazee, Steve; illustrated;
Authorized TV Adventure; 210 pgs.;
$12.00

❖LASSIE
The Mystery of Bristlecone Pine❖
#1505; 1967; Frazee, Steve; illustrated;
Authorized TV Edition; 214 pgs.; $10.00

❖LASSIE
The Secret of the Smelter's Cave❖
#1514; 1968; Frazee, Steve; illustrated;
Authorized TV Adventure; 210 pgs.; $12.00

❖LASSIE
The Wild Mountain Trail❖
#1513; 1966; Edmonds, I.G.; illus-
trated; Authorized TV Adventure;
214 pgs.; $15.00

❖LASSIE
Treasure Hunter❖
#1552; 1960; Strong, Charles S.; illustrated;
Authorized TV Edition; 282 pgs.; $14.00

❖LASSIE
Trouble At Panter's Lake❖
#1515; 1972; Frazee, Steve; illustrated;
Television Favorites; 210 pgs.; $12.00

❖LEAVE IT TO BEAVER❖
#1526; 1962; Fannin, Cole; illustrated; Autho-
rized TV Adventure; 210 pgs.; $40.00

(First aired 10/04/57 on CBS. In 1958 it was
picked up by ABC where it remained to
09/12/63. Starred Jerry Mathers as the
youngest of the Cleaver clan and the focus of
this sitcom.)

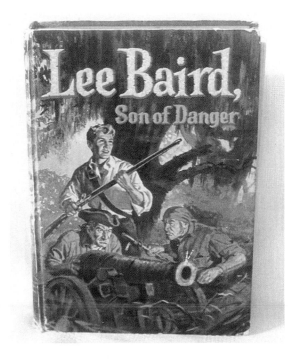

❖LEE BAIRD, SON OF DANGER
A Boy Fighter with Andrew Jackson❖
#1529; 1957; Thomas, H.C.; illustrated; Boys
Adventure; 282 pgs.; $10.00

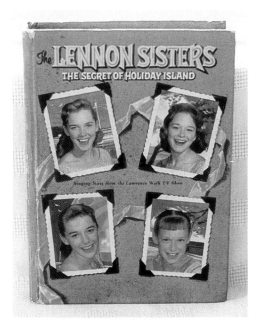

❖LENNON SISTERS, THE
The Secret of Holiday Island❖
#1544; 1960; Schroeder, Doris; illustrated;
Authorized TV Adventure; 282 pgs.; $10.00

(This copy has the standard TV logo on the
binding. The Lennon Sisters came to fame
through the Lawrence Welk Show where they
were featured as a singing act.)

❖LITTLE MEN❖
#2135; 1940; Alcott, Louisa
May; plain blue; (DJ); Whitman®
Classics; 234 pgs.; $12.00

❖LITTLE MEN❖
#2714; 1965; Alcott, Louisa
May; illustrated; Whitman® Classics Library; 252 pgs.; $5.00

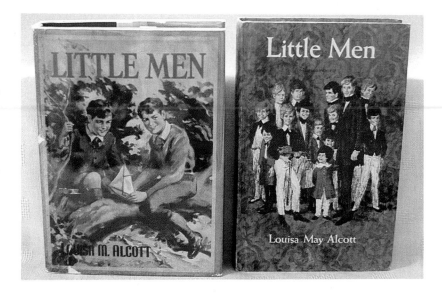

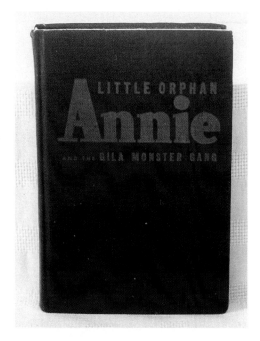

❖LITTLE ORPHAN ANNIE
And The Gila Monster Gang❖
#2302; 1944; Gray, Harold; plain blue; Authorized Edition; 248 pgs.; $22.00

(Gray's creation began in 1924 in the *New York News*. It has continued past Gray's death in 1968.)

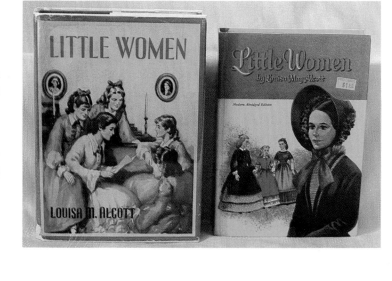

❖LITTLE WOMEN❖
No #; 1935; Alcott, Louisa May; plain blue; (DJ); Whitman® Classics Series; 237 pgs.; $16.00

❖LITTLE WOMEN❖
#1605; 1955; Alcott, Louisa May; illustrated; Whitman® Classics; 283 pgs.; $5.00

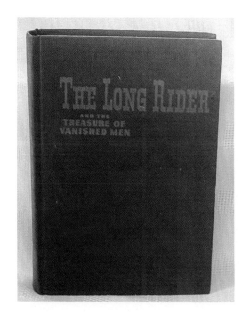

❖LONG RIDER, THE
And The Treasure of Vanished Men❖
#2317; 1946; Dubois, Gaylord; plain brown; Whitman® Authorized Edition; 248 pgs.; $16.00

❖LOST ON THE MOON
In Quest of the Field of Diamonds❖
#2347; 1911; Rockwood, Roy; plain lt. green;
Great Marvel Series; 248 pgs.; $20.00

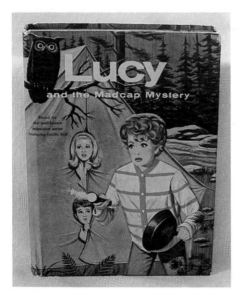

❖LUCY
And The Madcap Mystery❖
#1505; 1963; Fannin, Cole; illustrated; Authorized TV
Edition; 210 pgs.; $35.00

(From *The Lucy Show* on CBS. First aired 10/01/62.
Ran to 09/02/74. Starred Lucille Ball, Vivian Vance,
Charles Lane, Gale Gordon, Dick Martin, Candy Moore,
and Jimmy Garrett as Lucy Carmichael, Vivian Bagley,
Mr. Barnsdahl, Theodore J. Mooney, Henry Conners
and Chris and Jerry Carmichael.)

❖MAN FROM U.N.C.L.E., THE
The Affair of the Gunrunner's Gold❖
#1543; 1967; Keith, Brandon; illustrated;
Authorized TV Adventure; 212 pgs.; $18.00

(First aired 09/22/64 on NBC. Ran to
01/15/68. Starred Robert Vaughn and
David McCallum as Napoleon Solo and Illya
Kuryakin. Comic strip fantasy in an espi-
onage vein.)

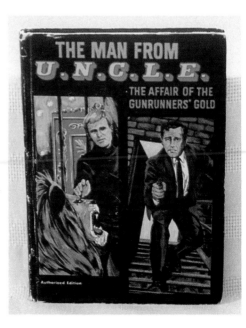

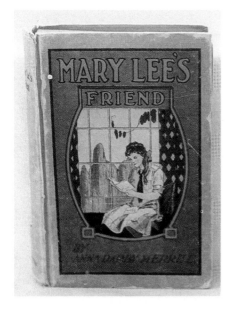

❖MARY LEE'S FRIEND❖
No #; 1920; Merrill, Anna Darby; illustrated; 218 pgs.; $13.00

❖MAVERICK❖
#1566; 1959; Coombs, Charles I.; illustrated; Authorized TV Adventure; 282 pgs.; $20.00

(First aired on ABC on 09/22/57. Ran to 07/08/62. Starred James Garner until 1960 as Brett Maverick. Jack Kelly played his brother Bart. Roger Moore also appeared for a season as Cousin Beauregard.)

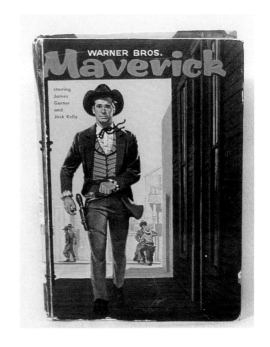

❖MEG
And The Disappearing Diamonds❖
#1759; 1967; Walker, Holly Beth; illustrated; Whitman® Tween Age Book; 156 pgs.; $8.00

❖MEG
And The Disappearing Diamonds❖
#1527; 1968; Walker, Holly Beth; illustrated; Whitman® Mystery; 136 pgs.; $6.00

❖MEG
The Ghost of Hidden Springs❖
#1530; 1970; Walker, Holly
Beth; illustrated; The Meg Mys-
teries; 138 pgs.; $8.00

❖MEG
The Mystery of the Black Magic Cave❖
#1506; 1971; Walker, Holly Beth; illustrated;
The Meg Mysteries; 138 pgs.; $8.00

❖MEG
The Secret of the Witch's Stairway❖
#1528; 1969; Walker, Holly Beth;
illustrated; The Meg Mysteries; 136
pgs.; $8.00

❖MEG
The Treasure Nobody Saw❖
#1529; 1970; Walker, Holly Beth; illustrated;
Whitman® Mystery; 136 pgs.; $8.00

❖MILESTONE SUMMER❖
#2311; 1962; Meridith, Nicolete; illus-
trated; Whitman® Teen Novel; 216 pgs.;
$8.00

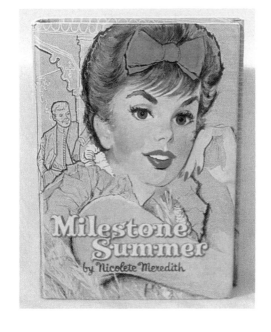

❖"MINNOW" VAIL❖
#1556; 1962; Wise, Winifred E.; illustrated;
Whitman® Novels For Girls; 212 pgs.;
$5.00

❖MISSION: IMPOSSIBLE
The Money Explosion❖
#1512; 1970; Powell, Talmage; illustrated; Authorized TV Adventure; 210 pgs.; $20.00

(Ran from 09/17/66 to 09/73 on CBS. Starred Steven Hill, Peter Graves, Barbara Bain, Martin Landau, Greg Morris and Peter Lupus. Adventure based on a team of government specialists assigned to duties too hazardous or impractical for the government to handle directly.)

❖MISSION: IMPOSSIBLE
The Priceless Particle❖
#1515; 1969; Powell, Talmage; illustrated; Authorized TV Adventure; 212 pgs.; $15.00

❖MOD SQUAD, THE
Assignment: The Arranger❖
#1538; 1969; Deming, Richard; illustrated; Authorized TV Adventure; 210 pgs.; $12.00

(First aired 09/24/68 on ABC. Ran to 08/23/73. Starred Michael Cole, Clarence Williams III and Peggy Lipton as Pete Cochran, Linc Hayes and Julie Barnes. A police drama featuring three troubled youths from differing backgrounds assigned to an undercover squad.)

❖MOD SQUAD, THE
Assignment: The Hideout❖
#1517; 1970; Deming, Richard; illustrated;
Authorized TV Adventure; 210 pgs.; $12.00

❖MONKEES, THE
Who's Got the Button?❖
#1539; 1968; Johnston, William; illustrated; Authorized TV Adventure; 208 pgs.;
$25.00

(First aired 09/12/66 on NBC. Ran to
08/19/68. Starred Davy Jones, Mickey
Dolenz, Peter Tork and Mike Nesmith as a
rock group cashing in on the success of
the Beatles' film, *A Hard Day's Night.*)

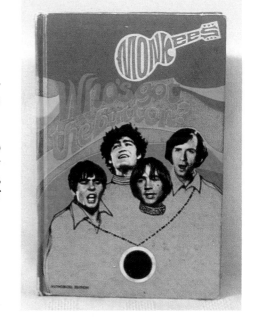

❖MORE TALES TO TREMBLE BY❖
#1629; 1968; Various; illustrated; Whitman®
Classics; 210 pgs.; $8.00

❖MORE THAN COURAGE Real Life Stories of
Horses and Dogs and People Who Have Loved
Them❖
#1513; 1960; Lawson, Patrick; illustrated;
Real Life Stories; 210 pgs.; $6.00

❖MOTHER GOOSE❖
#1682:79; 1953; Various; illustrated; Whit-
man® Giant Book; 315 pgs.; $10.00

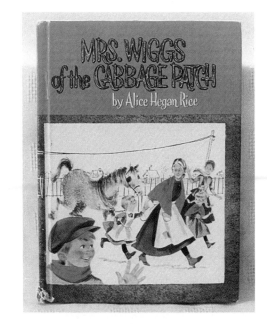

❖MRS. WIGGS
OF THE CABBAGE PATCH❖
#1602; 1962; Rice, Alice Hegan;
illustrated; Whitman® Classics; 138
pgs.; $5.00

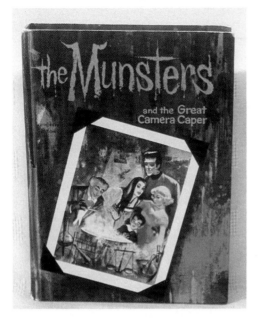

❖MUNSTERS, THE
And The Great Camera Caper❖
#1510; 1965; Johnston, William; illustrated;
Authorized TV Edition; 212 pgs.; $35.00

(First aired 09/24/64 on CBS. Ran to 09/01/66.
Starred Fred Gwynne and Yvonne DeCarlo as
Herman and Lily Munster. Sitcom based on a
family of creatures that looked like Famous
Monsters of Filmland and thought of themselves
as Ozzie and Harriet. Aired Thursday nights,
7:30 – 8:00.)

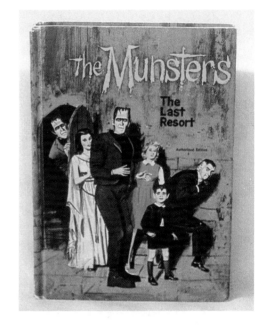

❖MUNSTERS, THE
The Last Resort❖
#1567; 1966; Johnston, William; illustrat-
ed; Authorized TV Adventure; 214 pgs.;
$25.00

❖MYSTERY AT RED TOP HILL❖
#1756; 1965; Schwaljie, Marjorie; illustrated;
Whitman® Tween Age Book; 154 pgs.; $4.00

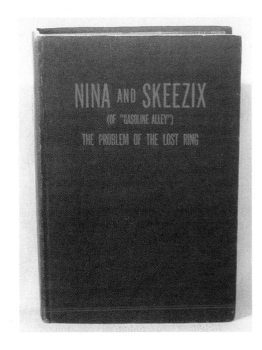

❖NINA AND SKEEZIX (of "Gasoline Alley") The Problem of the Lost Ring❖
#2377; 1942; King, Frank; plain brown; Authorized Edition; 248 pgs.; $10.00

❖NOAH CARR, YANKEE FIREBRAND
A Boy Sailor With John Paul Jones❖
#1534:49; 1957; Thomas, H.C.; illustrated; Young People's Fiction; 282 pgs.; $6.00

❖NORMA KENT OF THE WACS❖
#2392; 1943; Snell, Roy J.; plain brown; (DJ); Fighters For Freedom Series; 252 pgs.; $26.00

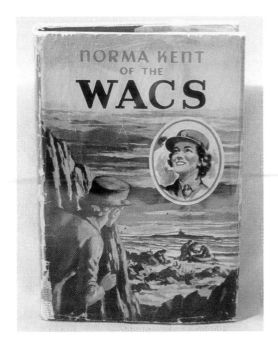

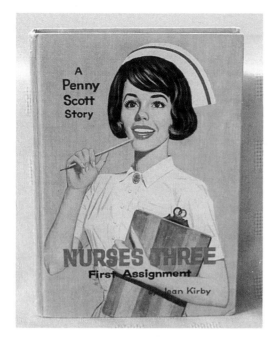

❖NURSES THREE
First Assignment, A Penny Scott Story❖
#2349; 1963; Kirby, Jean; illustrated; Books
For Girls; 216 pgs.; $10.00

❖NURSES WHO LED THE WAY;
Real Life Stories of Courageous Women
in an Exciting Profession❖
#1549; 1961; Various; illustrated; Real
Life Stories; 210 pgs.; $10.00

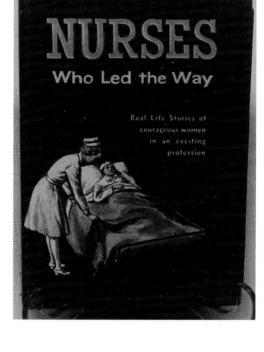

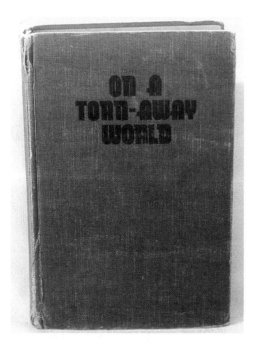

❖ON A TORN-AWAY WORLD
The Captives of the Great Earthquake❖
#2348; 1913; Rockwood, Roy; plain blue;
Great Marvel Series; 246 pgs.; $18.00

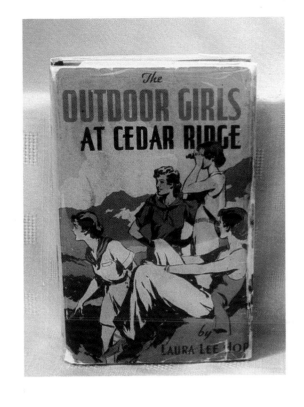

❖OUTDOOR GIRLS, THE
At Cedar Ridge❖
#2324; 1931; Hope, Laura Lee; plain red; (DJ);
Books For Girls; 214 pgs.; $16.00

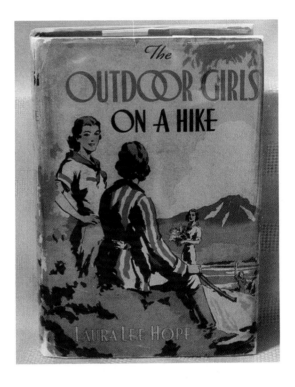

❖OUTDOOR GIRLS, THE
On a Hike❖
#2322; 1939; Hope, Laura Lee; plain red;
(DJ); Books For Girls; 236 pgs.; $15.00

❖PATTY DUKE
And Mystery Mansion❖
#1514; 1964; Schroeder, Doris; illustrat-
ed; Authorized TV Adventure; 212 pgs.;
$20.00

(First aired on ABC on 09/18/63. Ran
through 08/31/66. Starred Patty Duke
in a dual role as Patty and Cathy Lane.
Since they were identical, they often
switched places, much to the confusion
of those around them.)

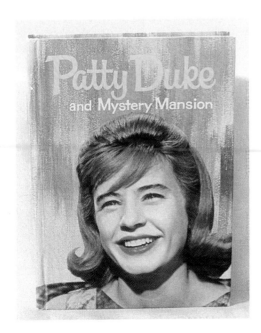

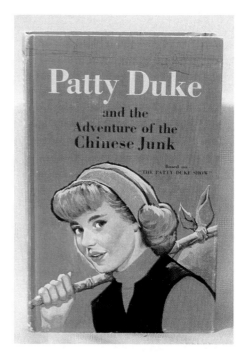

❖PATTY DUKE
And The Adventure of the Chinese Junk❖
#2334; 1966; Schroeder, Doris; illustrated;
Authorized TV Edition; 190 pgs.; $16.00

❖PEE-WEE HARRIS;
On the Trail❖
#2307; 1922; Fitzhugh, Percy K.; plain
gold; (DJ); Whitman® Books For Boys;
211 pgs.; $12.00

❖PEE-WEE HARRIS❖
#2306; 1922; Fitzhugh, Percy Keeze; plain
green; Pee-Wee Harris Series; 191 pgs.; $6.00

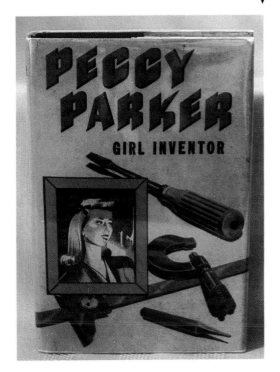

❖PEGGY PARKER;
Girl Inventor❖
#2328; 1946; Radford, Ruby Lorraine; plain blue;
(DJ); Authorized Edition; 248 pgs.; $18.00

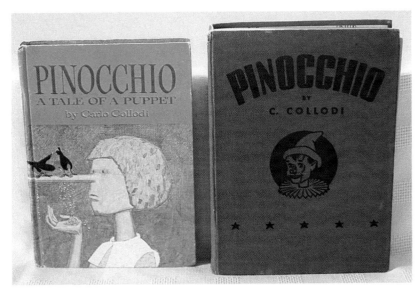

❖PINOCCHIO
A Tale of a Puppet❖ #1633;
1967; Collodi, Carlo; illustrated;
Whitman® Classics; 214 pgs.;
$5.00

❖PINOCCHIO❖
No #; 1916; Collodi, C.; plain
tan; Whitman® Classics; unp.;
$14.00

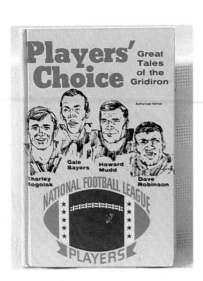

❖PLAYERS' CHOICE;
Great Tales of the Gridiron❖
#1535; 1969; Robinson, Mudd, Sayers
and Gogolak; illustrated; Sports Stories; 210 pgs.; $8.00

❖POLLY
In New York❖
#2364; 1922; Roy, Lillian Elizabeth; plain tan;
(DJ); Polly Brewster Series; 292 pgs.; $15.00

❖POLLY BREWSTER
Polly of Pebbly Pit❖ #2318; 1922; Roy,
Lillian; plain lt. green; Adventure For
Girls; 312 pgs.; $8.00

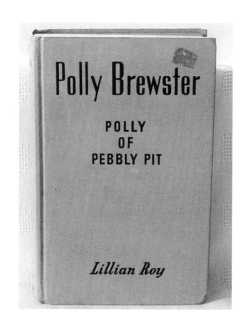

❖POLLY FRENCH
And The Surprising Stranger❖
#1572:49; 1956; Lewis, Francine; illustrated;
Whitman® Mystery Series; 282 pgs.; $8.00

❖POLLY FRENCH
Of Whitford High❖ #2364:49; 1954;
Lewis, Francine; illustrated; Girl's
Adventure; 282 pgs.; $8.00

❖POLLY FRENCH
Takes Charge❖
#1571:49; 1954; Lewis, Francine; illustrated;
Young People Fiction; 282 pgs.; $8.00

❖POLLY THE POWERS MODEL
The Puzzle of the Haunted Camera❖
#2375; 1942; Heisenfelt, Kathryn;
plain blue; (DJ); Authorized Edition;
246 pgs.; $22.00

(Features as heroine a girl from the
famous school for professional models
conducted by John Robert Powers.)

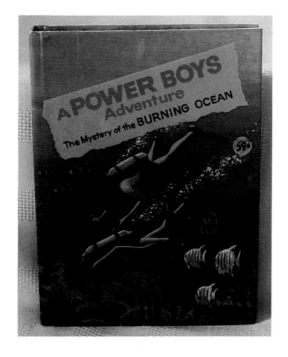

❖POWER BOYS ADVENTURE, A
The Mystery of the Burning Ocean❖
#1525; 1965; Lyle, Mel; illustrated; The Power
Boys Series; 210 pgs.; $8.00

❖POWER BOYS ADVENTURE, A
The Mystery of the Double Kidnapping❖
#1522; 1966; Lyle, Mel; illustrated;
Adventures; 208 pgs.; $7.00

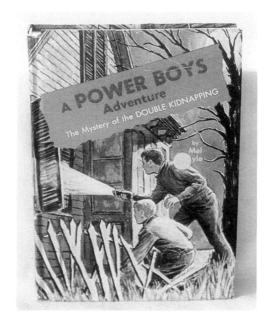

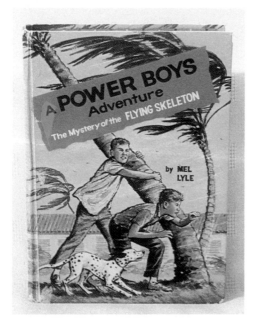

❖POWER BOYS ADVENTURE, A
The Mystery of the Flying Skeleton❖
#1524; 1964; Lyle, Mel; illustrated; Power
Boys Adventure Series; 210 pgs.; $10.00

❖POWER BOYS ADVENTURE, A
The Mystery of the Haunted Skyscraper❖
#1523; 1964; Lyle, Mel; illustrated; Power Boys
Adventure Series; 212 pgs.; $8.00

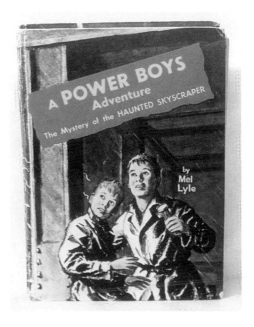

❖POWER BOYS ADVENTURE, A
The Mystery of the Million Dollar Penny❖
#1529; 1965; Lyle, Mel; illustrated; Power
Boys Series; 212 pgs.; $6.00

❖POWER BOYS ADVENTURE, A
The Mystery of the Vanishing Lady❖
#1526; 1967; Lyle, Mel; illustrated;
Power Boys Series; 214 pgs.; $5.00

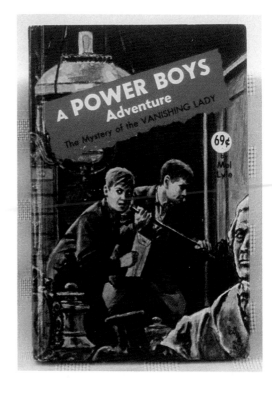

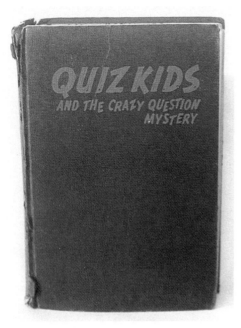

❖QUIZ KIDS
And The Crazy Question Mystery❖
#2332; 1946; Smith, Carl W.; plain blue; Whitman® Authorized Edition; 248 pgs.; $18.00

❖RAT PATROL, THE
The Iron Monster Raid❖
#1547; 1968; Edmonds, I.G.; illustrated; Authorized TV Adventure; 210 pgs.; $15.00

(First aired 09/12/66 on ABC. Ran to 09/16/68. Starred Chris George as Sgt. Sam Troy. War drama featuring a squad with jeeps fighting General Rommel in North Africa.)

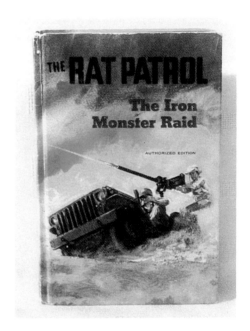

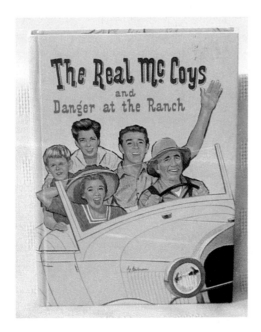

❖REAL MCCOYS, THE
And Danger at the Ranch❖
#1577; 1961; Fannin, Cole; illustrated; Authorized TV Adventure; 212 pgs.; $25.00

(First aired 10/03/57 on ABC. Ran to 09/62. Then picked up by CBS until 09/22/63. Starred Walter Brennan and Richard Crenna as Grandpa Amos and Luke McCoy. Sitcom based on an unsophisticated West Virginia family that moves to a San Fernando Valley ranch. Sound familiar?)

❖REBECCA OF SUNNYBROOK FARM❖
#2734; 1960; Wiggin, Kate Douglas;
illustrated; Whitman® Classics; 282
pgs.; $6.00

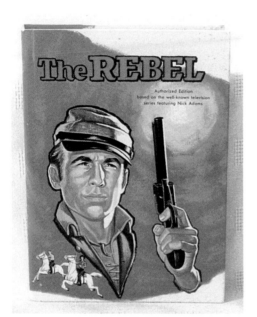

❖REBEL, THE❖
#1548; 1961; De Rosso, H.A.; illustrated;
Authorized TV Adventure; 212 pgs.; $20.00

(First aired 10/04/59 on ABC. Ran to
09/12/62. The episodes shown in 1962 were
run on NBC. Starred Nick Adams as Johnny
Yuma, an ex-Confederate soldier who wandered
from place to place on Sunday evenings from
9:00 to 9:30.)

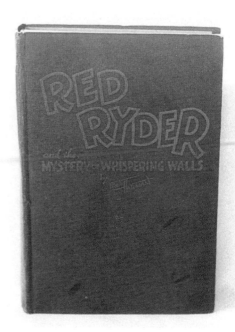

❖RED RYDER And The Mystery of
Whispering Walls❖
#2343; 1941; Harman, Fred; plain
blue; Authorized Edition; 220 pgs.;
$12.00

(Based on a highly typical western
strip penned by Fred Harman drawn
for the NEA service which appeared in
New York World Telegram.)

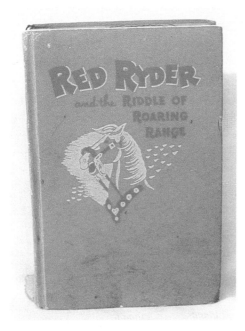

❖RED RYDER
And The Riddle of the Roaring Range❖
#2356; 1951; McGill, Jerry; plain
blue/green; Authorized Edition; 250
pgs.; $12.00

❖RED RYDER
And The Secret of the Lucky Mine❖
#2334; 1947; Smith, Carl; plain blue; (DJ);
Authorized Edition; 248 pgs.; $20.00

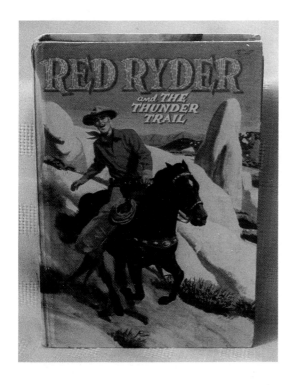

❖RED RYDER And The Thunder Trail❖
#1547:49; 1956; McGill, Jerry; illustrated;
Whitman® Authorized Edition; 282 pgs.;
$15.00

❖RESTLESS GUN, THE❖
#1559; 1959; Meyers, Barlow; illustrated; Authorized TV Edition; 282 pgs.; $25.00

(First aired on NBC 09/23/57 and ran through 09/14/59. Starred John Payne as Vint Bonner. A western based on the adventures of a gunfighter wandering across the Southwest after the Civil War.)

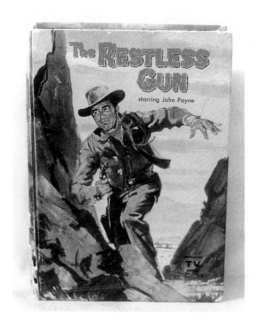

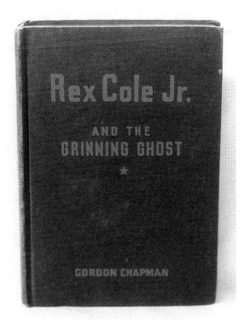

❖REX COLE JR. And The Grinning Ghost❖
#2311; 1931; Chapman, Gordon; plain brown; Boy's Fiction; 208 pgs.; $8.00

❖REX
King of the Deep❖
#2396; 1941; Dubois, Gaylord; plain dk. brown; (DJ); 1941; 214 pgs.; $10.00

(Based on a comic book story which appeared in *The Funnies* by Dell Publishing Company around 1940.)

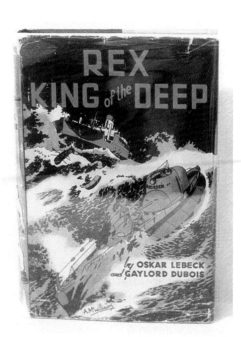

❖RIFLEMAN, THE❖
#1569; 1959; Fannin, Cole; illustrated; Authorized TV Adventure; 282 pgs.; $20.00

(First aired 09/30/58 on ABC. Ran to 07/01/63. Starred Chuck Conners and Johnny Crawford as Lucas and Mark McCain. Lucas McCain was a widowed rancher with a modified Winchester rifle. Needless to say, if he aimed at something, he hit it. A hit blend of tough guy and gentle father.)

❖RIN TIN TIN
And The Call To Danger❖
#1539; 1957; Schroeder, Doris; illustrated; Authorized TV Edition; 282 pgs.; $18.00

(Rin Tin Tin was the screen property of Warner Bros. He was known to exhibitors as the "Mortgage Lifter" due to his box office draw. Two successors followed him in the theaters and his lineal descendants appeared in the TV show. Starred Lee Aaker and James Brown as Rusty and Lt. Rip Masters. Sponsored by National Biscuit Company. First aired 10/15/54 on ABC. Ran to 08/28/59.)

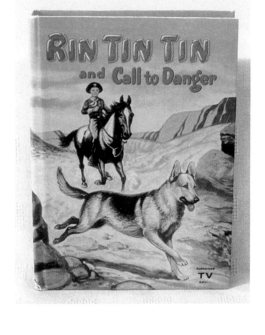

❖RIN TIN TIN
And The Ghost Wagon Train❖
#1579; 1958; Fannin, Cole; illustrated; Authorized TV Edition; 282 pgs.; $18.00

❖RIN TIN TIN
Rinty❖
#2362:49; 1954; Campbell, Julie; illustrated;
Authorized Edition; 282 pgs.; $20.00

❖RIP FOSTER
Assignment in Space With❖
#1576; 1958; Savage, Blake; illustrat-
ed; Whitman® Adventure Series; 282
pgs.; $12.00

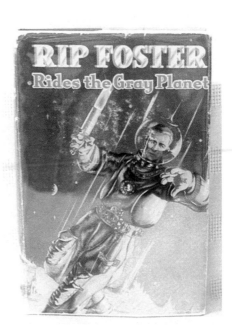

❖RIP FOSTER
Rides the Gray Planet❖
#2304; 1952; Savage, Blake; plain lt. blue;
(DJ); Adventure Series; 250 pgs.; $16.00

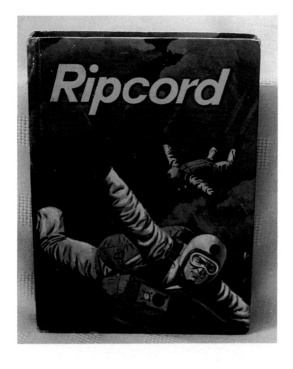

❖RIPCORD❖
#1522; 1962; Halacy, D.S.; illustrated; Authorized TV Adventure; 210 pgs.; $25.00

(A sydicated program, 76 episodes were produced from 9/61 to 1963. Starred Larry Pennell and Ken Curtis as Ted McKeever and Jim Buckley. Together they ran Ripcord Inc. and managed to skydive into and solve a variety of crimes, emergencies, and assorted situations.)

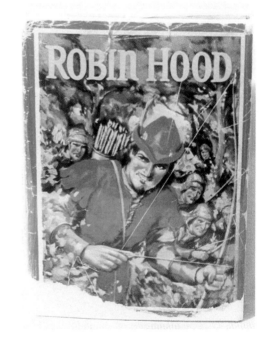

❖ROBIN HOOD❖
No #; 1940; Pyle, Howard; plain blue; (DJ); Whitman® Classics; 237 pgs.; $7.00

❖ROBIN KANE
Mystery in the Clouds❖
#1544; 1971; Hill, Eileen; illustrated; Whitman® Mystery; 188 pgs.; $8.00

❖ROBIN KANE
The Candle Shop Mystery❖
#1543; 1967; Hill, Eileen; illustrated;
Whitman® Mystery; 188 pgs.; $8.00

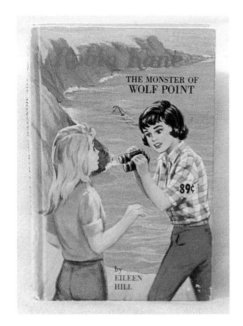

❖ROBIN KANE
The Monster of Wolf Point❖
#1546; 1971; Hill, Eileen; illustrated; Whit-
man® Mystery; 188 pgs.; $8.00

❖ROBIN KANE
The Mystery of Glengary Castle❖
#1552; 1966; Hill, Eileen; illustrated; Whit-
man® Mystery; 188 pgs.; $8.00

❖ROBIN KANE
The Mystery of the Blue Pelican❖
#1550; 1966; Hill, Eileen; illus-
trated; Whitman® Mystery; 188
pgs.; $8.00

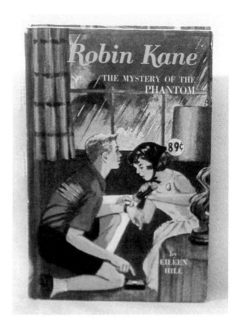

❖ROBIN KANE
The Mystery of the Phantom❖
#1551; 1966; Hill, Eileen; illustrated;
Whitman® Mystery; 188 pgs.; $8.00

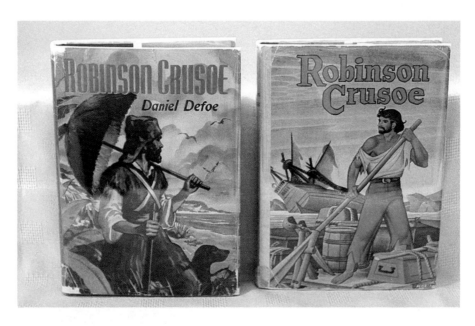

❖ROBINSON CRUSOE❖
#2124; n.d.; Defoe, Daniel; plain blue; (DJ); Whitman® Classics;
237 pgs.; $10.00

❖ROSE IN BLOOM❖
#1617; 1955; Alcott, Louisa May; illustrated; Whitman® Classics; 283 pgs.; $4.00

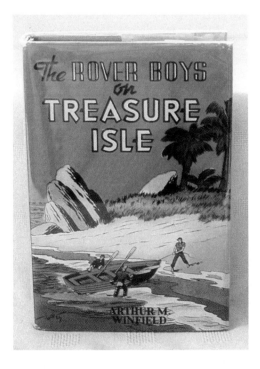

❖ROVER BOYS THE
On Treasure Isle❖
#2341; 1909; Winfield, Arthur M.; plain lt. green; (DJ); Rover Boys Series; 287 pgs.; $15.00

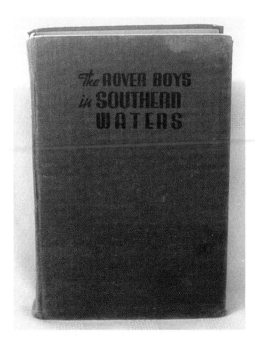

❖ROVER BOYS, THE
In Southern Waters❖
#2340; 1912; Winfield, Arthur M.; plain green; Rover Boys Series; 247 pgs.; $8.00

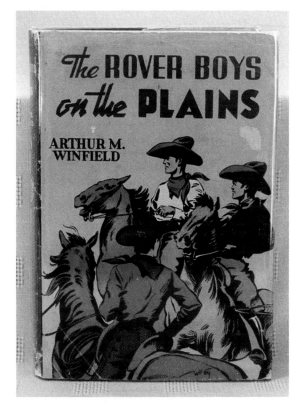

❖ROVER BOYS, THE
On the Plains❖
#2339; 1911; Winfield, Arthur M.;
plain green; (DJ); Rover Boys Series;
255 pgs.; $15.00

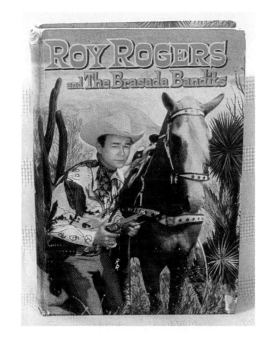

❖ROY ROGERS
And The Brasada Bandits❖ #1500:49;
1955; Fannin, Cole; illustrated; Whitman®
Authorized Edition; 282 pgs.; $25.00

(Ran from 12/30/51 on NBC to
06/23/57. Singing western star struggles
to bring law and order to everyone that
needs his help.)

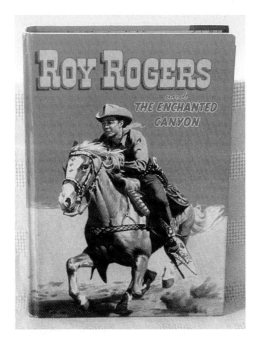

❖ROY ROGERS And The Enchanted Canyon❖
#1502:49; 1954; Rivers, Jim; illustrated;
Whitman® Authorized Edition; 282 pgs.;
$25.00

❖ROY ROGERS And The Ghost of Mystery Rancho❖
#2348; 1950; Tompkins, Walker A.; plain tan;
Whitman® Authorized Edition; 250 pgs.; $18.00

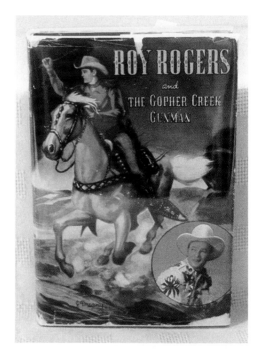

❖ROY ROGERS And The Gopher Creek
Gunman❖ #2309; 1945; Middleton, Don; plain
lt. blue; (DJ); Whitman® Authorized Edition;
248 pgs.; $30.00

❖ROY ROGERS
And The Raiders of Sawtooth Ridge❖
#2329; 1946; Miller, Snowden; plain
red; Authorized Edition; 246 pgs.;
$18.00

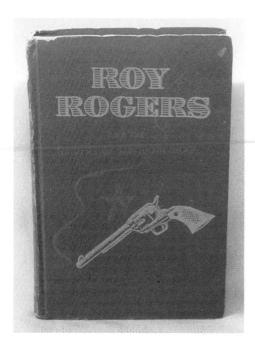

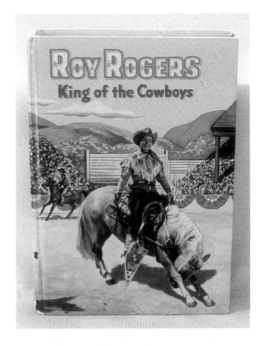

❖ROY ROGERS
King of the Cowboys❖
#1503:49; 1956; Fannin, Cole; illustrated; Whitman® Authorized Edition; 282 pgs.; $25.00

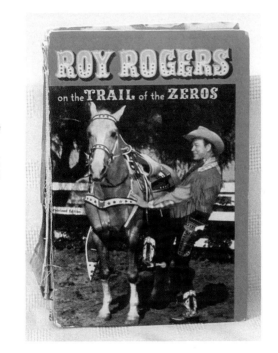

❖ROY ROGERS On The Trail of the Zeros❖
No #; 1954; Elton, Packer; illustrated; Authorized TV Edition; 282 pgs.; $35.00

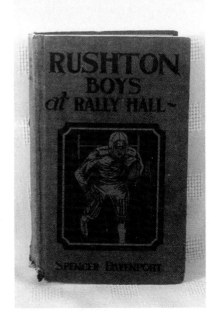

❖RUSHTON BOYS
At Rally Hall❖
No #; 1916; Davenport, Spencer; illustrated; Rushton Boys Series; 244 pgs.; $10.00

❖RUSHTON BOYS
At Treasure Cove❖
No #; 1916; Davenport, Spencer;
plain tan; Adventures For Boys; 246
pgs.; $10.00

(This book is in a smaller format. It
measures 4"x 6½".)

❖SADDLE PATROL❖
#1585; 1970; Rathjen, Carl Henry; illustrated;
Adventure Stories; 210 pgs.; $7.00

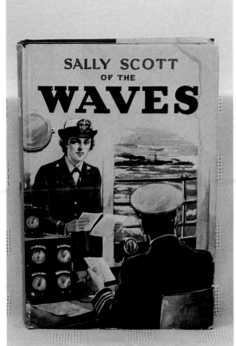

❖SALLY SCOTT Of the Waves❖
#2393; 1943; Snell, Roy J.; plain
green; (DJ); Fighters For Freedom;
248 pgs.; $25.00

❖SANDRA
Of the Girl Orchestra❖
#2321; 1946; Radford, Ruby Lorraine; plain green; Whitman® Authorized Edition; 248 pgs.; $14.00

❖WAY OUT
Science Fiction Adventure From❖
#1573; 1973; Various; illustrated; Whitman® Anthology; 212 pgs.; $8.00

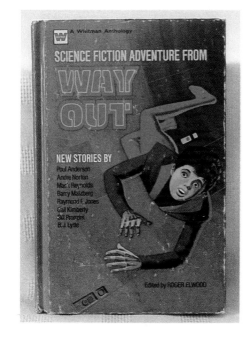

❖SEA HUNT❖
#1541; 1960; Fannin, Cole; illustrated; Authorized TV Adventure; 210 pgs.; $25.00

(Turned down by the networks, this show was produced in syndication from 1957-61. 156 episodes were made. The first was seen in January 1958. Starred Lloyd Bridges as Mike Nelson, an ex-Navy frogman turned undersea detective.)

❖SEVEN GREAT DETECTIVE STORIES❖
#1627; 1968; Various; illustrated;
Whitman® Classics; 210 pgs.; $6.00

❖SHIRLEY TEMPLE
And The Screaming Specter❖
#2330; 1946; Heisenfelt, Kathryn; plain green; Authorized Edition; 247 pgs.; $30.00

(Shirley Jane Temple was born in Santa Monica, California, on 4/23/29. She made her screen debut in 1932 in *Red Haired Alibi*. Made educational shorts until *Stand up and Cheer* in 1934 which resulted in her career as a child star. Voted one of the ten best money-making stars 1934-39.)

❖SHIRLEY TEMPLE
And The Spirit of Dragonwood❖
#2311; 1945; Heisenfelt, Kathryn; plain
brown; (DJ); Whitman® Authorized Edition; 248 pgs.; $25.00

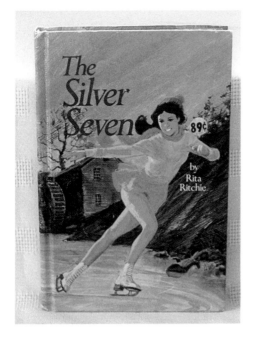

❖SILVER SEVEN, THE❖
#1548; 1972; Ritchie, Rita; illustrated; Whitman® Novel For Girls; 212 pgs.; $5.00

❖SMILIN' JACK
And The Daredevil Girl Pilot❖
#2379; 1942; Mosley, Zack; plain green; Comic Strip; 248 pgs.; $18.00

(Smilin' Jack first appeared on October 2, 1933 as a Sunday page and a daily strip in 1936. It then appeared in *Four Color Comics #5* in May 1940. *Four Color Comics* was published by the Dell Publishing Co.)

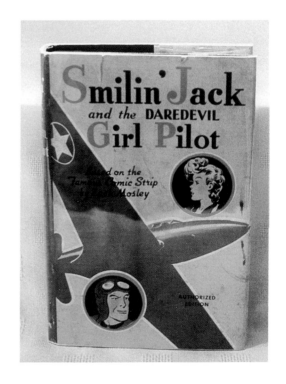

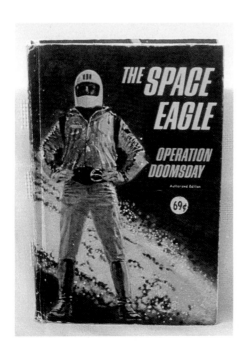

❖SPACE EAGLE, THE
Operation Doomsday❖
#1578; 1967; Pearl, Jack; illustrated; Adventure Series; 212 pgs.; $8.00

❖SPACE EAGLE, THE
Operation Star Voyage❖
#1579; 1970; Pearl, Jack; illustrated; Adventure Series; 208 pgs.; $5.00

❖SPIRIT TOWN❖
#1507; 1972; Roberts, Suzanne; illustrated;
Whitman® Novel For Girls; 212 pgs.; $8.00

❖STAND BY FOR ADVENTURE
Six Stories of Action❖
#1632; 1967; Various; illustrated;
Whitman® Classics; 212 pgs.; $5.00

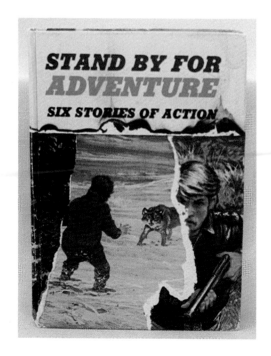

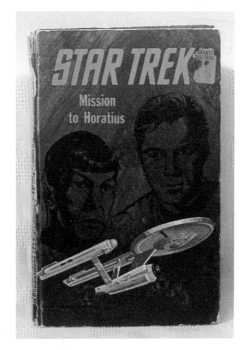

❖STAR TREK Mission to Horatius❖
#1549; 1968; Reynolds, Mack; illustrated;
Authorized TV Edition; 210 pgs.; $60.00

(First aired 09/08/66 on NBC. Ran to
09/02/69. Starred William Shatner, Leonard
Nimoy and DeForest Kelly as Capt. James
Tiberius Kirk, Mr. Spock and Dr. Leonard
McCoy.)

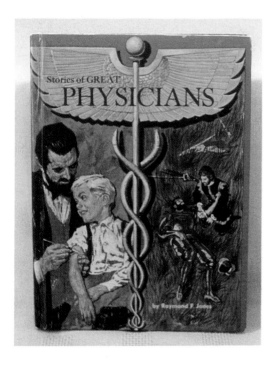

❖STORIES OF GREAT PHYSICIANS❖
#1581; 1963; Jones, Raymond F.;
illustrated; Real Life Stories; 210
pgs.; $4.00

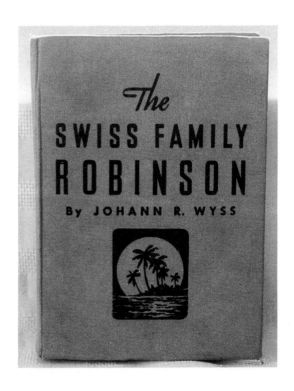

❖SWISS FAMILY ROBINSON, THE❖
No #; 1935; Wyss, Johann R.; plain lt. green;
Whitman® Classics; 235 pgs.; $4.00

❖SYLVIA SANDERS
And The Tangled Web❖
#2312; 1946; Radford, Ruby Lorraine; plain
brown; Authorized Edition; 248 pgs.; $16.00

❖TALES OF EDGAR ALLAN POE❖
#2701; 1963; Poe, Edgar Allan; illustrated;
Whitman® Classics; 282 pgs.; $6.00

❖TAMMY
Adventure in Hollywood❖
#2322; 1964; Wellman, Alice; illustrat-
ed; Authorized Edition; 214 pgs.;
$20.00

(This book is based on Ideal Toy Corp.
license which in turn is based on
Tammy of movie fame.)

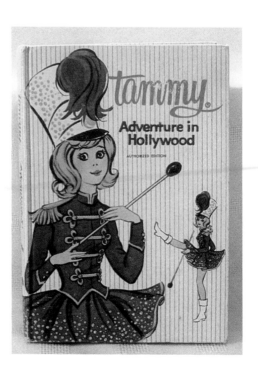

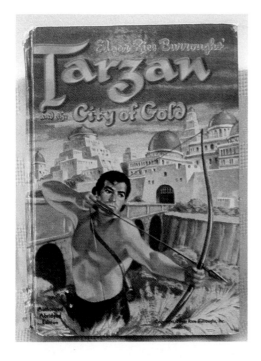

❖TARZAN
The City of Gold❖
#2307:49; 1954; Burroughs, Edgar Rice; illustrated; Authorized Edition; 282 pgs.; $15.00

❖TARZAN And The Forbidden City❖
#2306:49; 1954; Burroughs, Edgar Rice; illustrated; Whitman® Adventure Series; 282 pgs. ; $15.00

❖TARZAN And The Lost Safari❖
#1522:49; 1957; Burroughs, Edgar Rice; illustrated; Authorized Edition; 282 pgs.; $12.00

❖TARZAN
The Return of Tarzan❖
#1506; 1967; Burroughs, Edgar Rice; illustrated;
Whitman® Adventure Series; 214 pgs.; $10.00

❖TARZAN OF THE APES❖
#1507; 1964; Burroughs, Edgar Rice; illustrat-
ed; Authorized Edition; 285 pgs.; $20.00

❖TEN TALES CALCULATED TO GIVE
YOU SHUDDERS❖
#1617; 1972; Various; illustrated;
Whitman® Classics; 212 pgs.; $10.00

❖TERRY AND THE PIRATES ADVENTURE
April Kane and the Dragon Lady❖
#2380; 1942; Caniff, Milton; plain green; (DJ);
Whitman® Authorized Edition; 248 pgs.; $28.00

(Drawn by Milton Caniff, the strip was originally titled "Tommy Tucker" but the name was
changed to "Terry and the Pirates." Publication
began in October 1934.)

❖THAT CERTAIN GIRL❖
#1558; 1964; Snow, Dorothea J.; illus-
trated; Whitman® Novel For Girls; 216
pgs.; $7.00

❖THEN CAME NOVEMBER❖
#2346; 1963; Gilbert, Nan; illustrated; Whit-
man® Teen Novel; 286 pgs.; $6.00

❖THEY FLEW TO FAME❖
#1504; 1963; Bowen, Robert Sidney; illustrated;
Real Life Stories; 210 pgs.; $6.00

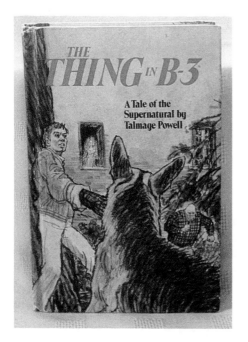

❖THING IN B-3, THE
A Tale of the Supernatural❖
#1581; 1969; Powell, Talmage; illustrated;
Adventure Stories; 210 pgs.; $5.00

❖THREE MATILDAS, THE
Make-Believe Daughter❖
#1502; 1972; Douglas, Laura W.; illus-
trated; Three Matildas Mystery; 212
pgs.; $4.00

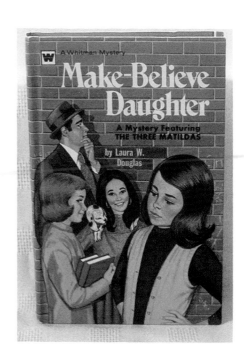

❖THREE MUSKETEERS❖
#2142; 1946; Dumas, Alexandre; plain block;
Whitman® Classics; 237 pgs.; $5.00

❖THROW THE LONG BOMB❖
#1536; 1967; Laflin, Jack; Foreword by
Bart Starr; illustrated; NFL Authorized
Edition; 214 pgs.; $6.00

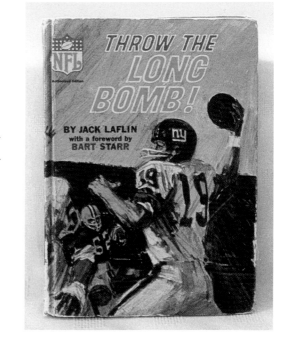

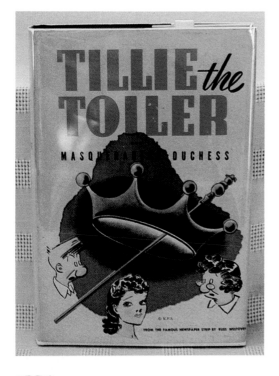

❖TILLIE THE TOILER
And The Masquerading Duchess❖
#2384; 1943; Westover, Russ; plain green;
(DJ); Whitman® Authorized Edition; 248 pgs.;
$25.00

(Based on comic strip penned by Russ Westover. Conceived in 1920, it first appeared in
1921 in the *New York American*. In 1927 a
feature film was made about her adventures.
The strip ended in 1959.)

❖TIMBER TRAIL RIDERS
The Long Trail North❖
#1593; 1963; Murray, Michael; illustrated;
Timber Trail Riders Series; 280 pgs.; $8.00

❖TIMBER TRAIL RIDERS
The Luck of Black Diamond❖
#1587; 1963; Murray, Michael; illus-
trated; Whitman® Adventure Series;
282 pgs.; $8.00

❖TIMBER TRAIL RIDERS
The Mysterious Dude❖
#1511; 1964; Murray, Michael; illustrated; Dave
Talbot Series; 280 pgs.; $8.00

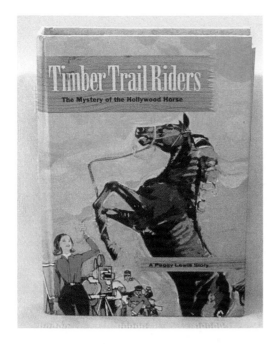

❖TIMBER TRAIL RIDERS
The Mystery of the Hollywood Horse❖
#1516; 1964; Murray, Michael; illustrated; A
Peggy Lewis Story; 280 pgs.; $8.00

❖TIMBER TRAIL RIDERS
The Texas Tenderfoot❖
#1588; 1963; Murray, Michael; illus-
trated; Whitman® Adventure Series;
282 pgs.; $8.00

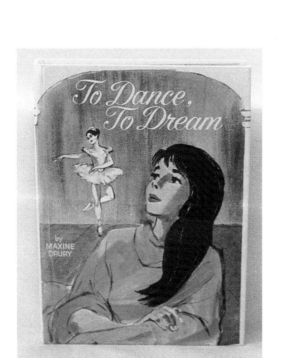

❖TO DANCE, TO DREAM❖
#1518; 1965; Drury, Maxine; illustrated;
Real Life Stories; 212 pgs.; $5.00

❖TOM SAWYER❖
#2127; 1944; Twain, Mark;
plain block; Whitman® Classics; 234 pgs.; $8.00

❖TOM SAWYER❖
#1603; 1955; Twain, Mark;
illustrated; Whitman® Classics; 284 pgs.; $5.00

❖TOM SAWYER❖
No #; 1931; Twain, Mark;
plain blue; Whitman® Classics;
unp.; $10.00

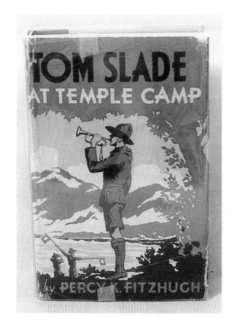

❖TOM SLADE
At Temple Camp❖
#2305; 1917; Fitzhugh, Percy K.; plain tan;
(DJ); Whitman® Books For Boys; 209 pgs.;
$20.00

❖TOM SLADE
Boy Scout❖ #2304; 1915; Fitzhugh,
Percy K.; plain tan; (DJ); Whitman®
Books For Boys; 206 pgs.; $25.00

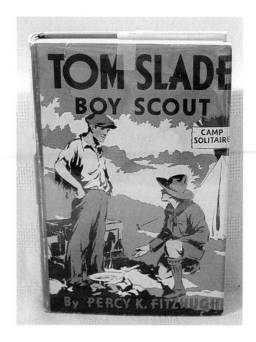

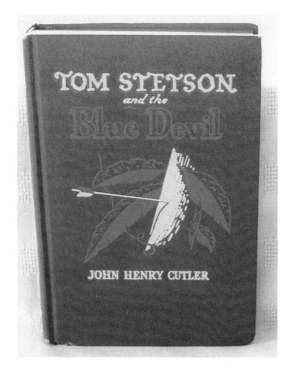

❖TOM STETSON
And The Blue Devil❖
#2358; 1951; Cutler, John Henry; plain
sienna; Whitman® Adventure; 248 pgs.;
$15.00

❖TOM STETSON
And The Giant Jungle Ants❖
#2340; 1948; Cutler, Henry; plain
brown; Authorized Edition; 248
pgs.; $12.00

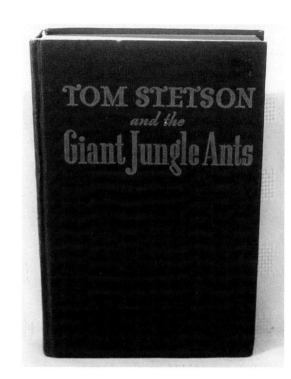

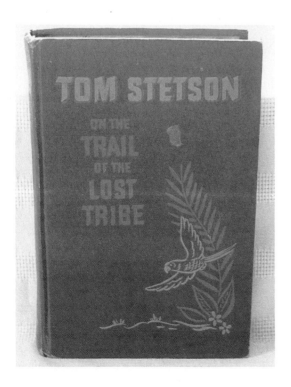

❖TOM STETSON
On the Trail of the Lost Tribe❖
#2341; 1948; Cutler, John Henry; plain
red; (DJ); Whitman® Adventure Series;
248 pgs.; $20.00

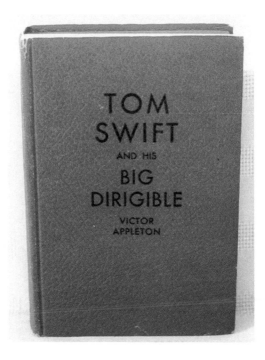

❖TOM SWIFT
And His Big Dirigible❖
No #; 1930; Appleton, Victor; plain tan;
214 pgs.; $12.00

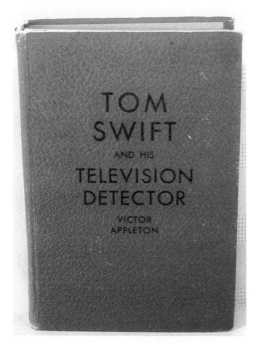

❖TOM SWIFT
And His Television Detector❖
No #; 1933; Appleton, Victor; plain dk. tan; Fic-
tion For Boys; 217 pgs.; $18.00

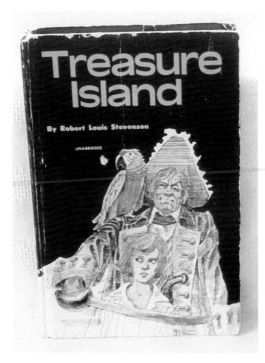

❖TREASURE ISLAND❖
#1610; 1971; Stevenson, Robert
Louis; illustrated; Whitman® Classics;
212 pgs.; $4.00

❖TRIXIE BELDEN®
And The Black Jacket Mystery❖
#2378; 1961; Kenny, Kathryn; illustrated; Trixie Belden® Series; 282 pgs.; $12.00

❖TRIXIE BELDEN®
And The Gatehouse Mystery❖
#1526; 1970; Campbell, Julie; illustrated; Whitman® Mystery; 234 pgs.; $8.00

❖TRIXIE BELDEN®
And The Happy Valley Mystery❖
#2307; 1962; Kenny, Kathryn; illustrated; Whitman® Mystery; 282 pgs.; $12.00

❖TRIXIE BELDEN®
And The Mystery at Bob-White Cave❖
#1586; 1971; Kenny, Kathryn; illustrated;
Whitman® Mystery; 212 pgs.; $8.00

❖TRIXIE BELDEN®
And The Mystery in Arizona❖
#1565; 1958; Campbell, Julie; illus-
trated; Trixie Belden® Mystery; 282
pgs.; $10.00

❖TRIXIE BELDEN®
And The Mystery of the Blinking Eye❖
#1587; 1971; Kenny, Kathryn; illustrated;
Whitman® Mystery; 212 pgs.; $8.00

❖TRIXIE BELDEN®
And The Mystery of the Emeralds❖
#2366; 1965; Kenny, Kathryn; illustrated;
Trixie Belden® Mystery; 254 pgs.;
$10.00

❖TRIXIE BELDEN®
And The Mystery off Glen Road❖
#1563; 1956; Campbell, Julie; illustrat-
ed; Trixie Belden® Series; 282 pgs.;
$15.00

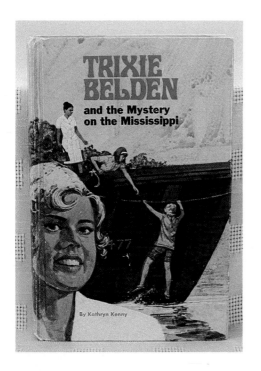

❖TRIXIE BELDEN®
And The Mystery on the Mississippi❖
#1523; 1971; Kenny, Kathryn; illustrated;
Whitman® Mystery; 234 pgs.; $8.00

❖TRIXIE BELDEN®
And The Red Trailer Mystery❖
No #; 1970; Campbell, Julie; illustrated; Whitman® Mystery; 236 pgs.; $8.00

❖TRIXIE BELDEN®
And The Secret of the Mansion❖
#1556; 1948; Campbell, Julie; illustrated; Whitman® Mystery; 282 pgs.; $18.00

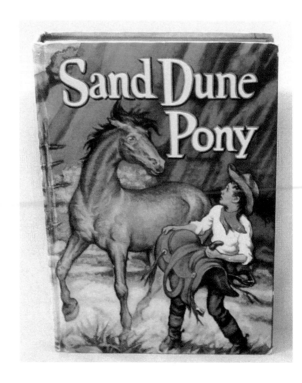

❖TROY NESBIT
Sand Dune Pony❖
#1544:49; 1954; Nesbit, Troy; illustrated; Troy Nesbit Mystery Adventures; 282 pgs.; $8.00

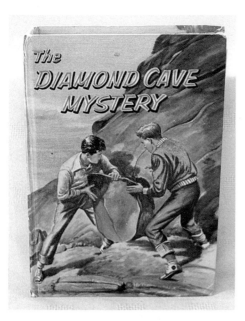

❖TROY NESBIT
The Diamond Cave Mystery❖
#1546:49; 1956; Nesbit, Troy; illustrated;
Adventures For Boys; 282 pgs.; $6.00

❖TROY NESBIT
The Forest Fire Mystery❖
#1527; 1962; Nesbit, Troy; illustrat-
ed; Troy Nesbit Series; 284 pgs.;
$5.00

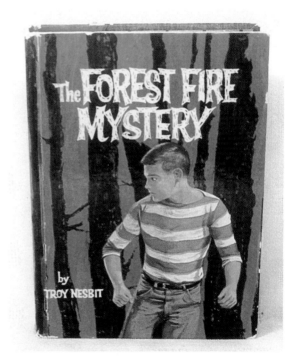

❖TROY NESBIT
The Indian Mummy Mystery❖ #1543:49;
1953; Nesbit, Troy; illustrated; Whitman®
Adventures for Boys; 282 pgs.; $10.00

❖TROY NESBIT
The Jinx of Payrock Canyon❖
#1545:49; 1954; Nesbit, Troy; illustrated;
Adventure Series; 282 pgs.; $8.00

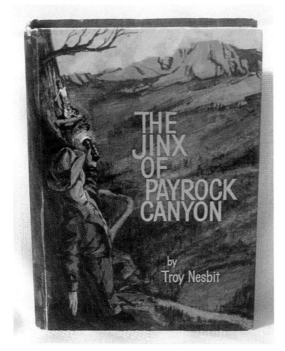

❖TROY NESBIT
The Jinx of Payrock Canyon❖
#1528; 1954; Nesbit, Troy; illustrated; Troy
Nesbit Series; 282 pgs.; $8.00

❖TROY NESBIT
The Mystery at Rustlers' Fort❖
#1533:49; 1957; Nesbit, Troy; illus-
trated; Troy Nesbit's Mystery Adventures; 282 pgs.; $8.00

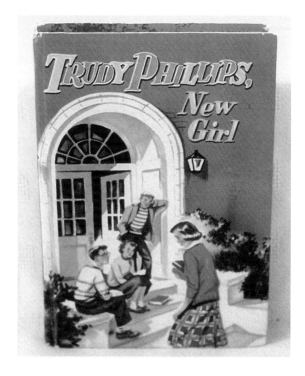

❖TRUDI PHILLIPS
New Girl❖
#1580; 1953; Bates, Barbara; illustrated; Girls
Adventure; 282 pgs.; $6.00

❖TRUE TO YOU❖
#1557; 1964; Rowe, Viola; illustrated;
Novel For Girls; 216 pgs.; $5.00

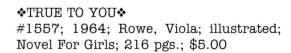

❖TUCKERS, THE
The Cottage Holiday❖
#2304; 1962; Mendel, Jo; illustrated; The
Tuckers Series; 282 pgs.; $10.00

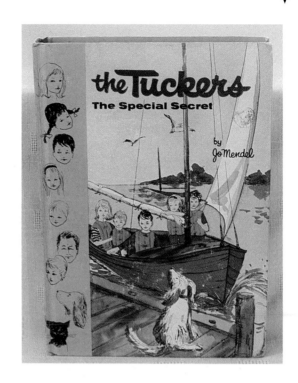

❖TUCKERS, THE
The Special Secret❖
#2301; 1961; Mendel, Jo; illustrated;
The Tuckers Series; 282 pgs.; $10.00

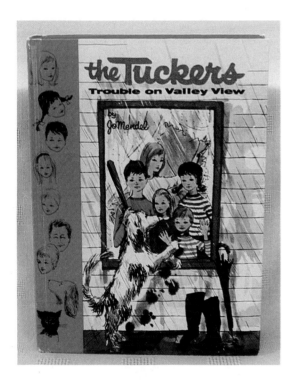

❖TUCKERS, THE;
Trouble on Valley View❖
#2303; 1956; Mendel, Jo; illustrated;
Tuckers Series; 282 pgs.; $10.00

❖VAN JOHNSON
The Luckiest Guy in the World❖
#2324; 1947; Beecher, Elizabeth; plain
green; Authorized Edition; 248 pgs.; $12.00

(Born in Newport, R.I., in 1916, Johnson
began his career in vaudeville. He did a stint
on the New York stage and first appeared on
screen in *Murder In Big House*. Voted one of
the top ten money-making stars for 1945-
46.)

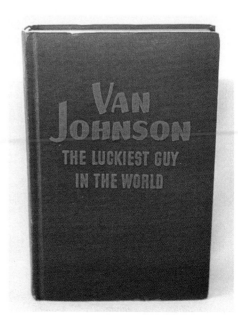

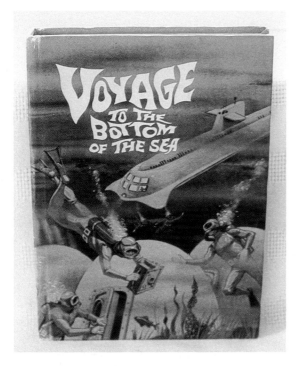

❖VOYAGE TO THE BOTTOM OF THE SEA❖
#1517; 1965; Jones, Raymond F.; illustrated;
Authorized TV Adventure; 212 pgs.; $25.00

(First aired 09/14/64 on ABC. Ran to
09/15/68. Starred Richard Basehart and David
Hedison as Adm. Nelson and Capt. Lee Crane.
Undersea adventure aboard the Seaview, an
atomic submarine.)

❖WAGON TRAIN❖
#1567; 1959; Nesbit, Troy; illustrated; Autho-
rized TV Adventure; 282 pgs.; $20.00

(First aired 09/18/57 on NBC. Ran to 09/62
when it was picked up by ABC from 09/62-
09/05/65. Starred Ward Bond and Robert Hor-
ton. This show helped signal the end of
anthology programming in favor of series with
recurring casts.)

❖WALT DISNEY'S ANNETTE
Mystery at Medicine Wheel❖
#1512; 1964; Meyers, Barlow; illustrated;
Authorized Edition; 212 pgs.; $12.00

❖WALT DISNEY'S ANNETTE
And The Mystery at Moonstone Bay❖
#1537; 1962; Schroeder, Doris; illustrated; Whitman Authorized Edition; 210 pgs.; $10.00

❖WALT DISNEY'S ANNETTE
Sierra Summer❖
#1585; 1960; Schroeder, Doris; illustrated; Whitman® Authorized Edition; 282 pgs.; $10.00

❖WALT DISNEY'S ANNETTE
The Desert Inn Mystery❖
#1546; 1961; Schroeder, Doris; illustrated; Whitman® Authorized Edition; 210 pgs.; $15.00

❖WALT DISNEY'S BEDKNOBS
AND BROOMSTICKS❖
#1570; 1971; Walsh and DaGradi; illustrated;
Whitman® Authorized Edition; 212 pgs.; $12.00

❖WALT DISNEY'S HANS BRINKER
Or The Silver Skates❖
#1601; 1961; Webb, Robert N.; illustrated; Whitman® Authorized Edition; 212
pgs.; $5.00

❖WALT DISNEY'S THE MISSADVENTURES
OF MERLIN JONES❖
#1521; 1964; Carey, Mary; illustrated; Authorized Edition; 210 pgs.; $10.00

(Based on a 1964 Disney comedy starring
Tommy Kirk and Annette Funicello. Concerned
the misadventures of a campus brain experimenting with hypnotism and mind-reading.)

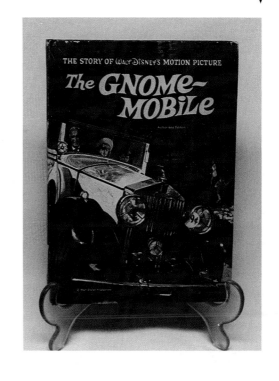

❖WALT DISNEY'S THE GNOME-MOBILE❖
#1577; 1967; Carey, Mary; illustrated; Whitman®
Authorized Edition; 140 pgs.; $12.00

(Based on the 1967 movie starring Walter Brennan, Matthew Garber, Karen Dotrice, Richard Deacon, Tom Lowell, Sean McClory, and Ed Wynn.)

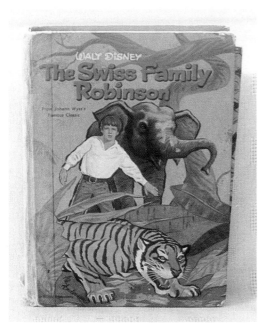

❖WALT DISNEY
The Swiss Family Robinson❖
#1625; 1960; Frazee, Steve; illustrated; Whitman® Authorized Edition; 210 pgs.; $8.00

(Based on the 1960 movie starring John Mills, Dorothy McGuire, James McArthur, Janet Munro, Tommy Kirk, Kevin Corcoran, and Sessue Hayakawa.)

❖WALT DISNEY'S TOBY TYLER❖
#1545; 1960; Snow, Dorothea J.; illustrated; Whitman® Authorized Edition;
282 pgs.; $10.00

❖WALT DISNEY'S ZORRO❖
#1586; 1958; Frazee, Steve; illustrated; Authorized TV Edition; 282 pgs.; $35.00

(First aired on ABC on 10/10/57. Ran to 09/24/59. Starred Guy Williams, George Lewis, Gene Sheldon, Britt Lomond, and Henry Calvin as Don Diego de la Vega (Zorro), Don Alejandro, Bernardo, Capt. Monastario, and Sgt. Garcia. Kind of an Hispanic Scarlet Pimpernel.)

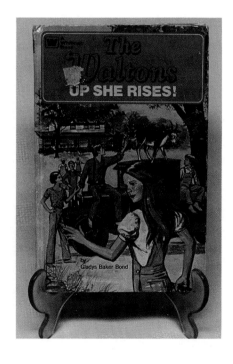

❖WALTONS, THE
Up She Rises!❖
#1539; 1975; Bond, Gladys Baker; illustrated; Whitman® TV Edition; 138 pgs.; $10.00

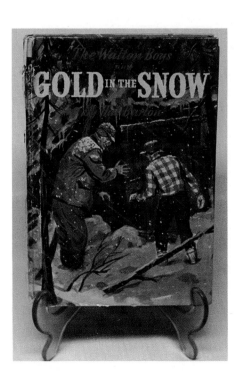

❖WALTON BOYS, THE And Gold in the Snow❖
#1522; 1958; Burton, Hal; illustrated; Walton Boys Series; 282 pgs.; $6.00

❖WALTON BOYS, THE
In High Country❖
#1523; 1960; Burton, Hal; illustrated;
Boy's Adventure Series; 282 pgs.; $5.00

❖WALTON BOYS, THE
In Rapids Ahead❖ #1525; 1958; Burton, Hal; illustrated; Whitman®
Adventure Series; 282 pgs.; $5.00

❖WALTON BOYS, THE
And Rapids Ahead❖
#2354; 1950; Burton, Hal; plain lt. green; (w/DJ and wo/DJ); Authorized
Edition; 248 pgs.; $8.00

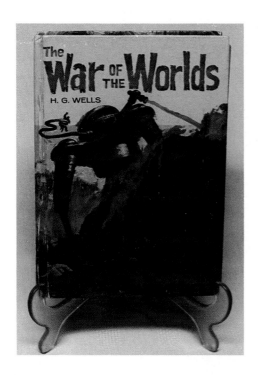

❖WAR OF THE WORLDS, THE❖
#1628; 1964; Wells, H.G.; illustrated;
Whitman® Classics; 280 pgs.; $12.00

❖WHEN DEBBIE DARED❖
#2325; 1963; Robinson, Kathleen; illus-
trated; Whitman® Teen Novel; 216 pgs.;
$5.00

❖WILD ANIMALS I HAVE KNOWN❖
#1619; 1961; Seton, Ernest Thompson; illus-
trated; Whitman® Classics; 283 pgs.; $6.00

❖WINNIE WINKLE
And The Diamond Heirlooms❖
#2319; 1946; Berke, Helen; plain blue; (DJ);
Whitman® Authorized Edition; 248 pgs.;
$28.00

(First appeared as a daily comic strip drawn
by Martin Michael Branner in the spring of
1920. The first career girl in comics and the
first to make use of contemporary fashions.
During the '40s her brother Perry temporarily
eclipsed her.)

❖WOLF OF THUNDER MOUNTAIN, THE
And Other Stories❖
#1580; 1970; Henderson, Dion; illustrated;
Whitman® Classics; 210 pgs.; $6.00

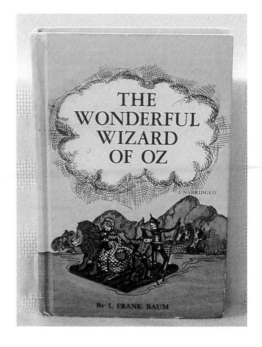

❖WONDERFUL WIZARD OF OZ, THE❖
#1620; 1970; Baum, Frank L.; illus-
trated; Whitman® Classics; 210 pgs.;
$5.00

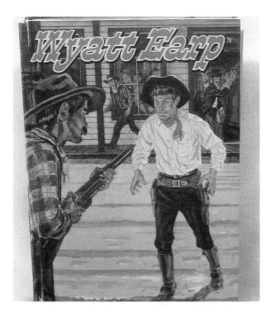

❖WYATT EARP❖
#1548; 1956; Ketchum, Philip; illustrated; Whitman® Adventure Series; 282 pgs.; $12.00

(This is a generic copy. It is not connected with the TV series.)

❖ZANE GREY'S
The Last Trail❖
#1526:49; 1954; Grey, Zane; illustrated; Young People Fiction; 282 pgs.; $10.00

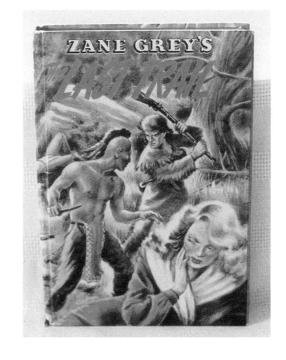

❖ZANE GREY'S
The Spirit of the Border❖
#2350:49; 1954; Grey, Zane; illustrated; Authorized Edition; 282 pgs.; $8.00

Books Not Pictured

ALGONQUIN; The Story of a Great Dog; #1618; 1953; Henderson, Dion; illustrated; Whitman® Classics; 211 pgs.; $4.00.

BLONDIE; Dagwood's Secret Service; #2374; 1942; Young, Chic; plain blue; Authorized Edition; 248 pgs.; $15.00.

CHEYENNE And The Lost Gold of Lion Park; #1587; 1958; Frazee, Steve; illustrated; Authorized TV Edition; 282 pgs.; $18.00.

First aired on ABC on 09/20/55. Ran to 09/13/63. Starred Clint Walker as Cheyenne Bodie. A post-Civil War western adventure drawn from the 1947 film starring Dennis Morgan. "Cheyenne" was one element of a triptych of shows in Warner Bros. Presents. One of the first one-hour adventure series.

HOUND OF THE BASKERVILLES, THE; #1624; 1968; Doyle, Sir Arthur Conan; illustrated; Whitman® Classics; 212 pgs.; $4.00.

GINNY GORDON And The Lending Library; #1551; 1954; Campbell, Julie; illustrated; Whitman® Mystery; 282 pgs; $8.00.

ROY ROGERS; The Outlaws of Sundown Valley; #2347; Miller, Snowden; plain blue; Authorized Edition; 250 pgs.; $25.00.

ROY ROGERS; The Rimrod Renegades; #2305; 1952; Miller, Snowden; plain blue; Authorized Edition; 250 pgs. $25.00.

ROY ROGERS & DALE EVANS; River of Peril; #1504; 1957; Fannin, Cole; plain tan; Authorized Edition; 282 pgs.; $25.00.

TOM SLADE; Boy Scout of the Moving Pictures; #2304; 1915; Fitzhugh, Percy Keeze; plain red; Boy's Books; 206 pgs.; $15.00.

TOM SWIFT and His Ocean Airport; #2164; 1934; Appleton, Victor; plain lt. green; Adventure For Boys; 214 pgs.; $12.00.

TRIXIE BELDEN® and The Marshland Mystery; #1578; 1971; Kenny, Kathryn; illustrated; Whitman® Mystery; 212 pgs.; $5.00.

TRIXIE BELDEN® and The Missing Heiress; #1542; 1970; Kenny, Kathryn; illustrated; Whitman® Mystery; 236 pgs.; $5.00.

TRIXIE BELDEN® and The Mysterious Code; #1540; 1970; Kenny, Kathryn; illustrated; Whitman® Mystery; 236 pgs.; $5.00.

TRIXIE BELDEN® and The Mysterious Visitor; #1532; 1970; Campbell, Julie; illustrated; Whitman® Mystery; 236 pgs.; $5.00.

TRIXIE BELDEN® and The Mystery on Cobbett's Island; #1521; 1971; Kenny, Kathryn; illustrated; Whitman® Mystery; 236 pgs; $5.00.

WALT DISNEY'S PETER PAN; #2132; 1952; Barrie, Sir James Matthew; block print; Authorized Edition; 188 pgs.; $14.00.

WALT DISNEY'S SPIN AND MARTY; Trouble At Triple-R; #1577; 1958; Schroeder, Doris; illustrated; Whitman® Authorized Edition; 282 pgs.; $25.00.

Spin and Marty was an episodic series featured on the Mickey Mouse Club which aired on ABC from 10/3/55 through 1959. Some of the shows were picked up as syndicated reruns in the early part of the '60s. Starred Tim Considine and David Stollery as Spin and Marty.

Books by Volume

- BETTER MAN, THE; 1910
- BUFFALO BILL The Boys' Friend; 1917
- CHRISTMAS STORIES; A Christmas Carol & Others; 1940
- LITTLE WOMEN; 1935
- MARY LEE'S FRIEND; 1920
- PINOCCHIO; 1916
- ROBIN HOOD; 1940
- ROY ROGERS On the Trail of the Zeros; 1954
- RUSHTON BOYS At Rally Hall; 1916
- RUSHTON BOYS At Treasure Cove; 1916
- SWISS FAMILY ROBINSON, The; 1935
- TOM SAWYER; 1931
- TOM SWIFT and His Big Dirigible; 1930
- TOM SWIFT And His Television Detector; 1933
- TRIXIE BELDEN® and The Red Trailer Mystery; 1970

554 – KIDNAPPED; 1935

1500 – LASSIE and The Secret of Summer; 1958

1500:49 – ROY ROGERS and The Brasada Bandits; 1955

1502 – THREE MATILDAS, THE; Make-Believe Daughter; 1972

1502:49 – ROY ROGERS and The Enchanted Canyon; 1954

1503 – DRAG STRIP DANGER; 1972

1503:49 – ROY ROGERS King of the Cowboys; 1956

1504 – LASSIE Lost In The Snow; 1969

1504 – ROY ROGERS AND DALE EVANS River of Peril; 1957

1504 – THEY FLEW TO FAME; 1963

1505 – LASSIE The Mystery of Bristlecone Pine; 1967

1505 – LUCY and The Madcap Mystery; 1963

1506 – CHALLENGE OF ICE Real Life Stories of Polar Explorers; 1963

1506 – TARZAN The Return of Tarzan; 1967

1506 – MEG The Mystery of the Black Magic Cave; 1971

1507 – SPIRIT TOWN; 1972

1507 – TARZAN OF THE APES; 1964

1508 – LASSIE Forbidden Valley; 1959

1509 – GYPSY FROM NOWHERE; 1972

1510 – MUNSTERS THE and the Great Camera Caper; 1965

1510:49 – GENE AUTRY The Ghost Riders; 1955

1511 – HAWAII FIVE-O Top Secret; 1969

1511 – TIMBER TRAIL RIDERS The Mysterious Dude; 1964

1511:49 – GENE AUTRY and The Golden Stallion; 1954

1512 – WALT DISNEY'S ANNETTE Mystery at Medicine Wheel; 1964

1512 – MISSION: IMPOSSIBLE The Money Explosion; 1970

1513 – MORE THAN COURAGE; 1960

1513 – LASSIE The Wild Mountain Trail; 1966

1514 – LASSIE The Secret of the Smelter's Cave; 1968

1514 – CHAMPIONS ALL THE WAY Real Life Stories of Outstanding Men and Women in the World of Sports; 1960

1514 – PATTY DUKE and Mystery Mansion; 1964

1515 – LASSIE Trouble At Panter's Lake; 1972

1515 – MISSION: IMPOSSIBLE The Priceless Particle; 1969

1515 – TROY NESBIT Sand Dune Pony; 1954

1516 – TIMBER TRAIL RIDERS The Mystery of the Hollywood Horse; 1964

1516 – LAND OF THE GIANTS Flight of Fear; 1969

1517 – VOYAGE TO THE BOTTOM OF THE SEA; 1965

1517 – MOD SQUAD, THE Assignment: The Hideout; 1970

1518 – TO DANCE TO DREAM; 1965

1519 – DR. KILDARE The Magic Key; 1964

1519 – HIGH CHAPARRAL The Apache Way; 1969

1520 – GUNSMOKE Showdown On Front Street; 1969

1520 – COMBAT The Counterattack; 1964

1521 – WALT DISNEY'S THE MISSADVENTURES OF MERLIN JONES; 1964

1521 – TRIXIE BELDEN® and The Mystery on Cobbett's Island; 1971

1521 – IRONSIDE The Picture Frame Frame-Up; 1969

1522 – RIPCORD; 1962

1522 – POWER BOYS Mystery, A, The Mystery of the Double Kidnapping; 1966

1522 – TRIXIE BELDEN® and The Mystery of the Emeralds; 1971

1522 – WALTON BOYS, THE and Gold in the Snow; 1958

1522:49 – TARZAN and The Lost Safari; 1957

1523 – GINNY GORDON and The Lending Library; 1971

1523 – POWER BOYS Mystery of the Haunted Skyscraper; 1964

1523 – TRIXIE BELDEN® and The Mystery on the Mississippi; 1971

1523 – WALTON BOYS in High Country; 1960

1524 – POWER BOYS Adventure, A, The Mystery of the Flying Skeleton; 1964

1525 – POWER BOYS Adventure, A, The Mystery of the Burning Ocean; 1965

1525 – WALTON BOYS, THE, The Rapids Ahead; 1958

1525:49 – ZANE GREY The Spirit of the Border; 1954

1526 – POWER BOYS Mystery of the Vanishing Lady; 1967

1526 – TRIXIE BELDEN® and The Gatehouse Mystery; 1970

1526 – LEAVE IT TO BEAVER; 1962

1526:49 – ZANE GREY'S The Last Trail; 1954

1527 – MEG and The Disappearing Diamonds; 1968

1527 – TROY NESBIT The Forest Fire Mystery; 1962

1527 – DRAGNET Case Stories; 1957

1528 – MEG, and The Secret of the Witch's Stairway; 1969

1528 – TROY NESBIT and The Jinx of Payrock Canyon; 1954

1529 – POWER BOYS Mystery of the Million Dollar Penny; 1965

1529 – LEE BAIRD, Son of Danger, A Boy Fighter With Andrew Jackson; 1957

1529 – MEG and The Treasure Nobody Saw; 1970

1530 – MEG and The Ghost of Hidden Springs; 1970

1530 – BOBBSEY TWINS, THE, In the Country; 1953

1531 – FAMILY NAME, THE; 1971

1531 – BOBBSEY TWINS, THE, Merry Days Indoors and Out; 1950

1532 – TRIXIE BELDEN® and The Mysterious Visitor; 1970

1533 – TRIXIE BELDEN® and Mystery in Arizona; 1970

1533:49 – TROY NESBIT The Mystery at Rustlers' Fort; 1957

1534 – TRIXIE BELDEN® and The Mystery off Glen Road; 1970

1534:49 – NOAH CARR, YANKEE FIREBRAND, A Boy Sailor With John Paul Jones; 1957

1535 – PLAYERS' CHOICE Great Tales of the Gridiron; 1969

1536 – THROW THE LONG BOMB; 1967

1536 – LASSIE and the Mystery At Blackberry Bog; 1956

1536 – JANET LENNON Adventure at Two Rivers; 1961

1537 – WALT DISNEY'S ANNETTE and The Mystery At Moonstone Bay; 1962

1537 – BASKET FEVER; 1970

1537 – FURY and The Lone Pine Mystery; 1957

1538 – MOD SQUAD, THE Assignment: The Arranger; 1969

1539 – RIN TIN TIN and The Call To Danger; 1957

1539 – MONKEES, THE Who's Got the Button?; 1968

1539 – JANET LENNON at Camp Calamity; 1962

1539 – WALTONS, THE Up She Rises; 1975

1540 – TRIXIE BELDEN® and The Mysterious Code; 1970

1540 – DONNA PARKER Mystery at Arawak; 1962

1540:49 – ANNIE OAKLEY In Danger At Diablo; 1955

1541 – TRIXIE BELDEN® and The Black Jacket Mystery; 1970

1541 – SEA HUNT; 1960

1541 – MAN FROM U.N.C.L.E., THE, The Affair of the Gentle Saboteur; 1966

1542 – TRIXIE BELDEN® and The Missing Heiress; 1970

1542 – I SPY Message From Moscow; 1966

1543 – ROBIN KANE The Candle Shop Mystery; 1967

1543 – MAN FROM U.N.C.L.E., THE, The Affair of the Gunrunners' Gold; 1967

1543:49 – TROY NESBIT The Indian Mummy Mystery; 1953

1544 – LENNON SISTERS, THE, The Secret of Holiday Island; 1960

1544 – ROBIN KANE Mystery In the Clouds; 1971

1544 – F TROOP The Great Indian Uprising; 1967

1544:49 – TROY NESBIT Sand Dune Pony; 1954

1545 – INVADERS, THE Dam of Death; 1967

1545 – WALT DISNEY'S TOBY TYLER; 1960

1545:49 – TROY NESBIT and The Jinx of Payrock Canyon; 1954

1546 – WALT DISNEY'S ANNETTE The Desert Inn Mystery; 1961

1546 – ROBIN KANE The Monster of Wolf Point; 1971

1546:49 – TROY NESBIT The Diamond Cave Mystery; 1956

1546:49 – TROY NESBIT The Diamond Cave Mystery; 1956

1547 – DR. KILDARE Assigned To Trouble; 1963

1547 – RAT PATROL, THE, The Iron Monster Raid; 1968

1547:49 – RED RYDER and The Thunder Trail; 1956

1548 – WYATT EARP; 1956

1548 – GARRISON'S GORILLAS and The Fear Formula; 1968

1548 – SILVER SEVEN, THE; 1972

1548 – REBEL, THE; 1961

1549 – CIRCUS BOY Under the Big Top; 1957

1549 – NURSES WHO LED THE WAY Real Life Stories of Courageous Women in an Exciting Profession; 1961

1549 – STAR TREK Mission To Horatius; 1968

1550 – BAT MASTERSON; 1960

1550 – ROBIN KANE The Mystery of the Blue Pelican; 1966

1551 – ROBIN KANE The Mystery of the Phantom; 1966

1551 – GINNY GORDON and The Lending Library; 1954

1552 – LASSIE Treasure Hunter; 1960

1552 – ROBIN KANE The Mystery of Glengary Castle; 1966

1553 – HAWAII FIVE-O The Octopus Caper; 1971

1554 – DIVERS DOWN Adventure Under Hawaiian Seas; 1971

1554:49 – GINNY GORDON and The Broadcast Mystery; 1956

1555 – CHARMED CIRCLE, THE; 1962

1555 – GINNY GORDON and The Broadcast Mystery; 1956

1556 – TRIXIE BELDEN® and The Secret of the Mansion; 1948

1556 – "MINNOW" VAIL; 1962

1557 – FURY and The Mystery at Trapper's Hole; 1959

1557 – TRUE TO YOU; 1964

1558 – THAT CERTAIN GIRL; 1964

1559 – RESTLESS GUN, THE; 1959

1561 – BRAINS BENTON Mystery, A, The Case of the Counterfeit Coin; 1960

1562 – BRAINS BENTON Mystery, A, The Case of the Stolen Dummy; 1961

1563 – BRAINS BENTON Mystery, A, The Case of the Roving Rolls; 1961

1563 – TRIXIE BELDEN® and The Mystery off Glen Road; 1956

1564 – FAMOUS INVESTIGATORS;1963

1565 – TRIXIE BELDEN® and Mystery in Arizona; 1958

1565 – BRAINS BENTON Case of the Painted Dragon; 1961

1566 – GILLIGAN'S ISLAND; 1966

1566 – MAVERICK; 1959

1567 – FAMILY AFFAIR Buffy Finds a Star; 1970

1567 – MUNSTERS, THE, The Last Resort; 1966

1567 – WAGON TRAIN; 1959

1568 – BONANZA Killer Lion; 1966

1568 – HAVE GUN, WILL TRAVEL; 1959

1569 – BIG VALLEY, THE; 1966

1569 – RIFLEMAN, THE; 1959

1570 – GREEN HORNET, THE, The Case of the Disappearing Doctor; 1966

1570 – WALT DISNEY'S BEDKNOBS & BROOMSTICKS; 1971

1571 – BICYCLES NORTH A Mystery On Wheels; 1973

1571:49 – POLLY FRENCH Takes Charge; 1954

1572 – BEVERLY HILLBILLIES, THE, The Saga of Wildcat Creek; 1963

1572 – BEWITCHED The Opposite Uncle; 1970

1572:49 – POLLY FRENCH and The Surprising Stranger; 1956

1573 – SCIENCE FICTION ADVENTURE FROM WAY OUT;1973

1574 – CELLAR TEAM; 1972

1575 – GINNY GORDON and The Disappearing Candlesticks; 1954

1576 – RIP FOSTER Assignment In Space with; 1958

1577 – REAL MCCOYS, THE Danger at the Ranch; 1961

1577 – WALT DISNEY'S THE GNOME-MOBILE; 1967

1577 – WALT DISNEY'S SPIN AND MARTY Trouble At Triple-R; 1958

1578 – CIRCUS BOY War On Wheels; 1958

1578 – TRIXIE BELDEN® and The Marshland Mystery; 1971

1578 – SPACE EAGLE, THE Operation Doomsday; 1967

1579 – SPACE EAGLE, THE Operation Star Voyage; 1970

1579 – RIN TIN TIN and The Ghost Wagon Train; 1958

1579 – GREAT WAR, THE Stories of World War I; 1965

1580 – TRUDI PHILLIPS New Girl; 1953

1580 – HEROES IN BLUE AND GRAY; 1965

1580 – WOLF OF THUNDER MOUNTAIN, THE and Other Stories; 1970

1580:49 – TRUDI PHILLIPS New Girl; 1953

1581 – STORIES OF GREAT PHYSICIANS; 1963

1581 – THING IN B-3, THE A Tale of the Supernatural; 1969

1582 – HOT ROD ROAD; 1968

1583 – JANET LENNON and The Angels; 1963

1585 – SADDLE PATROL; 1970

1585 – WALT DISNEY'S ANNETTE Sierra Summer; 1960

1586 – TROY NESBIT The Diamond Cave Mystery; 1964

1586 – TRIXIE BELDEN® and The Mystery at Bob-White Cave; 1971

1587 – TIMBER TRAIL RIDERS and The Luck of Black Diamond; 1963

1587 – TRIXIE BELDEN® and The Mystery of the Blinking Eye; 1971

1586 – WALT DISNEY'S ZORRO; 1958

1587 – CHEYENNE and The Lost Gold of Lion Park; 1958

1588 – TIMBER TRAIL RIDERS and The Texas Tenderfoot; 1963

1589 – DONNA PARKER Takes A Giant Step; 1954

1590 – DONNA PARKER At Cherrydale; 1957

1591 – DONNA PARKER Special Agent; 1957

1592 – DONNA PARKER On Her Own; 1957

1593 – DONNA PARKER In Hollywood; 1956

1593 – TIMBER TRAIL RIDERS and The Long Trail North; 1963

1594 – DONNA PARKER A Spring To Remember; 1960

1595 – KIM ALDRICH Mystery, A, Miscalculated Risk; 1972

1596 – KIM ALDRICH Mystery, A, Silent Partner; 1972

1601 – WALT DISNEY's HANS BRINKER or The Silver Skates; 1961

1602 – MRS. WIGGS OF THE CABBAGE PATCH; 1962

1603 – TOM SAWYER; 1955

1604 – BLACK BEAUTY; 1955

1605 – LITTLE WOMEN; 1955

1606 – HUCKLEBERRY FINN; 1955

1608 – HEIDI Grows Up; 1971

1609 – FAMOUS FAIRY TALES; 1971

1609 – FIVE LITTLE PEPPERS and How They Grew; 1955

1609:49 – FIVE LITTLE PEPPERS and How They Grew; 1955

1610 – TREASURE ISLAND; 1971

1612:49 – ADVENTURES OF SHERLOCK HOLMES; 1955

1613 – FRECKLES; 1961

1616 – ALICE IN WONDERLAND; 1970

1617 – ROSE IN BLOOM; 1955

1617 – TEN TALES CALCULATED TO GIVE YOU SHUDDERS; 1972

1618 – ALGONQUIN The Story of a Great Dog; 1953

1618 – EIGHT COUSINS; 1955

1619 – WILD ANIMALS I HAVE KNOWN; 1961

1620 – WONDERFUL WIZARD OF OZ, THE; 1970

1621 – THREE MUSKETEERS, THE; 1956

1621 – ADVENTURE CALLING Nine Great Stories of the Outdoors; 1969

1622 – BIOGRAPHY OF A GRIZZLY AND LOBO, THE; 1969

1623 – A BATCH OF THE BEST Stories For Girls; 1970

1624 – HOUND OF THE BASKERVILLES, THE; 1968

1625 – BEAUTIFUL JOE; 1955

1625 – WALT DISNEY The Swiss Family Robinson; 1960

1627 – SEVEN GREAT DETECTIVE STORIES; 1968

1628 – WAR OF THE WORLDS, THE; 1964

1629 – MORE TALES TO TREMBLE BY; 1968

1632 – STAND BY FOR ADVENTURE Six Stories of Action; 1967

1633 – PINNOCCHIO A Tale of a Puppet; 1967

1635 – CALL OF THE WILD, THE; 1970

1682:79 – MOTHER GOOSE; 1953

1753 – GOLDEN PRIZE and Other Stories About Horses; 1965

1754 – KENNY AND HIS ANIMAL FRIENDS; 1965

1755 – ADVENTURES WITH HAL; 1965

1756 – MYSTERY AT RED TOP HILL; 1965

1757 – IT'S A MYSTERY! Stories of Suspense; 1965

1759 – MEG and The Disappearing Diamonds; 1967

1760 – DORY BOY; 1966

2106 – FAVORITE STORIES;A Collection of the Best-loved Tales of Childhood; 1968

2121 – HEIDI; 1944

2124 – ROBINSON CRUSOE; n.d.

2127 – TOM SAWYER; 1944

2129 – FIFTY FAMOUS AMERICANS; 1946

2132 – WALT DISNEY'S PETER PAN; 1952

2135 – LITTLE MEN; 1940

2142 – THREE MUSKETEERS; 1946

2144 – CHRISTMAS STORIES; 1951

2164 – TOM SWIFT and His Ocean Airport; 1934

2300 – BLONDIE and Dagwood's Adventure In Magic; 1944

2300 – BOBBY BLAKE At Rockledge School; 1915

2301 – BOBBY BLAKE At Bass Cove or The Hunt For the Motor Boat Gem; 1915

2301 – JANE WITHERS and The Swamp Wizard; 1944

2301 – TUCKERS, THE The Special Secret; 1961

2302 – LITTLE ORPHAN ANNIE and The Gila Monster Gang; 1944

2302 – ANDY LANE 15 Days in The Air; 1928

2302:49- GENE AUTRY and The Big Valley Grab; 1954

2303 – TUCKERS, THE Trouble On Valley View; 1956

2303 – GENE AUTRY and The Thief River Outlaws; 1944

2304 – RIP FOSTER Rides the Gray Planet; 1952

2304 – TOM SLADE Boy Scout; 1915

2304 – TOM SLADE Boy Scout of the Moving Pictures; 1915

2304 – TUCKERS, THE, The Cottage Holiday; 196

2305 – KITTY CARTER Canteen Girl; 1944

2305 – ROY ROGERS and The Rimrod Renegades; 1952

2305 – TOM SLADE At Temple Camp; 1917

2306 – BETTY GRABLE and The House of Cobwebs; 1947

2306 – PEE-WEE HARRIS 1922

2306:49 – TARZAN and The Forbidden City; 1954

2307 – TRIXIE BELDEN® and The Happy Valley Mystery; 1962

2307 – DICK DONNELLY of the Paratroops; 1944

2307 – PEE-WEE HARRIS On the Trail; 1922

2307:49 – TARZAN and The City of Gold; 1954

2308 – JUDY GARLAND and The Hoodoo Costume; 1945

2309 – ROY ROGERS and The Gopher Creek Gunman; 1945

2310 – DICK TRACY Meets the Night Crawler; 1945

2310 – DEFIANT HEART, THE; 1964

2311 – SHIRLEY TEMPLE and The Spirit of Dragonwood; 1945

2311 – REX COLE JR. and The Grinning Ghost; 1931

2311 – MILESTONE SUMMER; 1962

2312 – HAL KEEN Hermit of Gordon's Creek; 1931

2312 – SYLVIA SANDERS and The Tangled Web; 1946

2313 – BLUE STREAK and Doctor Medusa; 1946

2314 – A BOY SAILOR WITH JOHN PAUL JONES; 1946

2317 – LONG RIDER, THE and the Treasure of Vanished Men; 1946

2318 – POLLY BREWSTER Polly of Pebbly Pit; 1922

2319 – WINNIE WINKLE and The Diamond Heirlooms; 1946

2320 – BLYTHE GIRLS, THE Helen, Margy and Rose; 1925

2320 – KING OF THE ROYAL MOUNTED and The Ghost Guns of Roaring River; 1946

2321 – SANDRA of The Girl Orchestra; 1946

2322 – OUTDOOR GIRLS, THE On a Hike; 1939

2322 – TAMMY Adventure In Hollywood; 1964

2324 – "FLIPPER" The Mystery of the Black Schooner; 1966

2324 – OUTDOOR GIRLS, THE At Cedar Ridge; 1931

2324 – VAN JOHNSON The Luckiest Guy In the World; 1947

2325 – WHEN DEBBIE DARED; 1963

2326 – GENE AUTRY and The Redwood Pirates; 1946

2327 – DON WINSLOW and The Scorpion's Stronghold; 1946

2328 – PEGGY PARKER Girl Inventor; 1946

2329 – ROY ROGERS and The Raiders of Sawtooth Ridge; 1946

2330 – SHIRLEY TEMPLE and The Screaming Specter; 1946

2331 – A BOY FIGHTER WITH ANDREW JACKSON; 1946

2332 – QUIZ KIDS The Crazy Question Mystery; 1946

2332 – BOBBSEY TWINS THE, At The Seashore, 1954

2334 – PATTY DUKE and The Adventure of the Chinese Junk; 1966

2334 – RED RYDER and The Secret of the Old Lucky Mine; 1947

2339 – ROVER BOYS, THE On the Plains; 1911

2340 – ROVER BOYS, THE In Southern Waters; 1912

2340 – TOM STETSON and The Giant Jungle Ants; 1948

2341 – TOM STETSON On the Trail of the Lost Tribe; 1948

2341 – ROVER BOYS, THE On Treasure Isle; 1909

2342 – BOBBSEY TWINS, THE, Merry Days Indoors and Out; 1950

2343 – RED RYDER Mystery of Whispering Walls; 1941

2345 – FIVE THOUSAND MILES UNDERGROUND; 1913

2346 – THEN CAME NOVEMBER; 1963

2347 – LOST ON THE MOON In Quest of the Field of Diamonds; 1911

2347 – ROY ROGERS Outlaws of Sundown Valley; 1950

2348 – ON A TORN-AWAY WORLD The Captives of the Great Earthquake; 1913

2348 – ROY ROGERS and The Ghost of Mystery Rancho; 1950

2349 – NURSES THREE First Assignment, A Penny Scott Story; 1963

2349 – GENE AUTRY and The Golden Ladder Gang; 1950

2350:49 – ZANE GREY'S The Spirit of the Border; 1954

2351 – BERT WILSON AT PANAMA; 1940

2352 – GINNY GORDON and The Missing Heirloom; 1950

2354 – WALTON BOYS, THE in The Rapids Ahead; 1950

2355 – TRIXIE BELDEN® and The Mystery At Bob-White Cave; 1963

2355 – DEANNA DURBIN The Adventure of Blue Valley; 1941

2355 – GENE AUTRY and The Badmen of Broken Bow; 1951

2356 – DEANNA DURBIN and The Feather of Flame; 1941

2356 – RED RYDER and The Riddle of the Roaring Range; 1951

2358 – TOM STETSON and The Blue Devil; 1951

2358 – JOY AND PAM; 1927

2360 – JOY AND PAM At Brookside; 1929

2362 – JUDY JORDAN'S DISCOVERY; 1931

2362:49- RIN TIN TIN Rinty, 1954

2364 – POLLY In New York; 1922

2364:49 – POLLY FRENCH of Whitford High; 1954

2366 – TRIXIE BELDEN® and The Mystery of the Emeralds; 1965

2369 – TRIXIE BELDEN® and The Gatehouse Mystery; 1959

2371 – BONITA GRANVILLE and The Mystery of Star Island; 1942

2371:49 – GENE AUTRY and The Golden Stallion; 1954

2372 – ANN RUTHERFORD and The Key To Nightmare Hall; 1942

2374 – BLONDIE and Dagwood's Secret Service; 1942

2375 – POLLY THE POWERS MODEL The Puzzle of the Haunted Camera; 1942

2376 – JOYCE OF THE SECRET SQUADRON A Captain Midnight Adventure; 1942

2377 – NINA AND SKEEZIX (of "Gasoline Alley") The Problem of the Lost Ring; 1942

2378 – GINGER ROGERS and The Riddle of the Scarlet Cloak; 1942

2378 – TRIXIE BELDEN® and The Black Jacket Mystery; 1961

2379 – SMILIN' JACK and The Daredevil Girl Pilot; 1942

2380 – TERRY AND THE PIRATES Adventure, A, April Kane and the Dragon Lady; 1942

2381 – DICK TRACY Ace Detective; 1943

2382 – INVISIBLE SCARLET O'NEIL; 1943

2383 – BRENDA STARR Girl Reporter; 1943

2384 – TILLIE THE TOILER and The Masquerading Duchess; 1943

2385 – JOHN PAYNE and The Menace at Hawk's Nest; 1943

2386 – BETTY GRABLE and The House with the Iron Shutters; 1943

2387 – BOOTS and The Mystery of the Unlucky Vase; 1943

2388 – BLONDIE and Dagwood's Snapshot Clue; 1943

2389 – JANE WITHERS and the Phantom Violin; 1943

2390 – ANN SHERIDAN and The Sign of the Sphinx; 1943

2392 – NORMA KENT OF THE WACS; 1943

2393 – SALLY SCOTT OF THE WAVES; 1943

2394 – BARRY BLAKE of The Flying Fortress; 1943

2396 – REX King of the Deep; 1941

2701 – TALES OF EDGAR ALLAN POE; 1963

2712 – BEAUTIFUL JOE; 1965

2713 – FRECKLES; 1961

2714 – LITTLE MEN; 1965

2717 – ADVENTURES OF SHERLOCK HOLMES; 1965

2719 – HUCKLEBERRY FINN; 1965

2734 – REBECCA OF SUNNYBROOK FARM; 1960

4059 – BLUE BOOK OF CHILDREN'S STORIES, THE; 1934

Books by Author

Ackworth, Robert C.;
DR. KILDARE; Assigned To Trouble

Adams, Eustace L.;
ANDY LANE; 15 Days In the Air

Alcott, Louisa May;
EIGHT COUSINS
LITTLE MEN
LITTLE WOMEN
ROSE IN BLOOM

Alter, Robert E.;
HEROES IN BLUE AND GRAY

Appleton, Victor;
TOM SWIFT and His Big Dirigible
and His Ocean Airport
and His Television Detector

Barrie, Sir James Matthew;
WALT DISNEY'S PETER PAN

Bates, Barbara;
TRUDI PHILLIPS; New Girl

Baum, Frank L.;
WONDERFUL WIZARD OF OZ, THE

Beecher, Elizabeth;
VAN JOHNSON; The Luckiest Guy In the World

Berke, Helen;
WINNIE WINKLE and The Diamond Heirlooms

Bingham, Mildred;
IT'S A MYSTERY!; Stories of Suspense

Bond, Gladys Baker;
ADVENTURES WITH HAL
FAMILY AFFAIR; Buffy Finds a Star
WALTONS, THE; Up She Rises

Bowen, Robert Sidney;
BASKET FEVER
HAWAII FIVE-O; Top Secret
THEY FLEW TO FAME

Brady, Cyrus Townsend;
BETTER MAN, THE; With Some Account of What
He Struggled For and What He Won

Burroughs, Edgar Rice;
TARZAN and The City of Gold
and The Forbidden City
and the Lost Safari
THE RETURN OF TARZAN
TARZAN OF THE APES

Burton, Hal;
WALTON BOYS, THE; In High Country

In Rapids Ahead
Gold in the Snow

Campbell, Julie;
GINNY GORDON and The Lending Library
and The Broadcast Mystery
and The Disappearing Candlesticks
and The Missing Heirloom
TRIXIE BELDEN® and the Gatehouse Mystery
and The Mysterious Visitor
and The Mystery in Arizona
and The Mystery off Glen Road
and The Red Trailer Mystery
and The Secret of The Mansion
RIN TIN TIN; Rinty

Caniff, Milton;
TERRY AND THE PIRATES Adventure, April Kane
and the Dragon Lady

Carey, Mary;
WALT DISNEY'S the MISSADVENTURES OF
MERLIN JONES
WALT DISNEY'S THE GNOME-MOBILE

Carroll, Lewis;
ALICE IN WONDERLAND

Chapman, Gordon;
REX COLE JR. and The Grinning Ghost

Collodi, Carlo
PINNOCCHIO; A Tale of a Puppet

Coombs, Charles I.;
MAVERICK

Cutler, Henry;
TOM STETSON and The Giant Jungle Ants

Cutler, John Henry;
TOM STETSON On the Trail of the Lost Tribe
and The Blue Devil

Davenport, Spencer;
RUSHTON BOYS; At Rally Hall
At Treasure Cove

Davis, Franklin M. Jr.; COMBAT; The Counterattack

Defoe, Daniel; ROBINSON CRUSOE

Deming, Richard; DRAGNET; Case Stories
FAMOUS INVESTIGATORS
MOD SQUAD, THE;
Assignment: The Arranger;
Assignment: The Hideout

De Rosso, H.A.; REBEL, THE

Dickens, Charles; CHRISTMAS STORIES; A Christmas
Carol & Others

Douglas, Laura W.; THREE MATILDAS, THE; Make-Believe Daughter

Doyle, A. Conan; ADVENTURES OF SHERLOCK HOLMES
HOUND OF THE BASKERVILLES, THE

Drury, Maxine; TO DANCE, TO DREAM

DuBois, Gaylord; BARRY BLAKE of the Flying Fortress
REX; King of the Deep
LONG RIDER, THE and The Treasure of Vanished Men

Duffield, J.W.; BERT WILSON AT PANAMA

Dumas, Alexandre; THREE MUSKETEERS

Duncan, Gregory; DICK DONNELLY of the Paratroops

Edmonds, I.G.; LASSIE; The Wild Mountain Trail
RAT PATROL, THE; The Iron Monster Raid

Elder, Art; BLUE STREAK and Doctor Medusa

Ellis, Leo R.; HAWAII FIVE-O; The Octopus Caper

Elton, Packer; ROY ROGERS on the Trail of the Zeros

Fannin, Cole; GENE AUTRY and The Golden Stallion
LEAVE IT TO BEAVER
LUCY and the Madcap Mystery
REAL MCCOYS, THE; and Danger at the Ranch
RIFLEMAN, THE
RIN TIN TIN and The Ghost Wagon Train
ROY ROGERS; King of the Cowboys
The Brasada Bandits
ROY ROGERS AND DALE EVANS; River of Peril
SEA HUNT

Fenton, William; FURY and The Lone Pine Mystery

Fitzhugh, Percy K.; PEE-WEE HARRIS; On the Trail;
TOM SLADE; At Temple Camp Boy Scout
Boy Scout
Boy Scout of the Moving Pictures

Frazee, Steve; BONANZA; Killer Lion
CHEYENNE and The Lost Gold of Lion Park
HIGH CHAPARRAL; The Apache Way
LASSIE; Lost In The Snow
The Mystery of Bristlecone Pine
The Secret of the Smelter's Cave
Trouble At Panter's Lake
WALT DISNEY; The Swiss Family Robinson
WALT DISNEY'S ZORRO

Garis, Lilian; JUDY JORDAN'S DISCOVERY

Gilbert, Nan; THEN CAME NOVEMBER

Gordon, Hal; DIVERS DOWN; Adventure Under Hawaiian Seas

Gould, Chester; DICK TRACY; Ace Detective Meets the Night Crawler

Gray, Harold; LITTLE ORPHAN ANNIE and The Gila Monster Gang

Greiner, N. Gretchen and Wiliam H. Larson; ADVENTURE CALLING; Nine Great Stories of the Outdoors

Grey, Zane; The KING OF THE ROYAL MOUNTED and the Ghost Guns of Roaring River
The Last Trail
The Spirit of the Border

Griffith, Ward; FIFTY FAMOUS AMERICAN

Halacy, D.S.; RIPCORD

Hamilton, Bob; GENE AUTRY and The Redwood Pirates;
and The Thief River Outlaws

Hardwick, Richard; "FLIPPER"; The Mystery of the Black Schooner

Harman, Fred; RED RYDER and The Mystery of Whispering Walls

Hecklemann, Charles; BIG VALLEY, THE

Heisenfelt, Kathryn; ANN RUTHERFORD and The Key To Nightmare Hall
ANN SHERIDAN and The Sign of the Sphinx
BETTY GRABLE and The House of Cobwebs
The House with the Iron Shutters
BONITA GRANVILLE and The Mystery of Star Island
DEANNA DURBIN; Feather of Flame
The Adventure of Blue Valley
JANE WITHERS and The Swamp Wizard
JOHN PAYNE and The Menace at Hawk's Nest
JUDY GARLAND and The Hoodoo Costume
POLLY THE POWERS MODEL; The Puzzle of the Haunted Camera
SHIRLEY TEMPLE; The Spirit of Dragonwood
The Screaming Specter

Henderson, Dion; ALGONQUIN; The Story of a Great Dog
WOLF OF THUNDER MOUNTAIN, THE

Hill, Eileen;
ROBIN KANE; Mystery In the Clouds
The Candle Shop Mystery
The Monster of Wolf Point
The Mystery of Glengary Castle
The Mystery of the Blue Pelican
The Mystery of the Phantom

Hope, Laura Lee; BLYTHE GIRLS, THE; Helen, Margy and Rose
    BOBBSEY TWINS, THE;
            In the Country
            Merry Days Indoors and Out
            At the Seashore
    OUTDOOR GIRLS, THE; On a Hike
            At Cedar Ridge

Hutchinson, W.H.; GENE AUTRY and The Golden Ladder Gang
    and the Big Valley Grab

Jablonski, Edward; GREAT WAR, THE; Stories of World War I

Johnston, William; BEWITCHED; The Opposite Uncle
    DR. KILDARE; The Magic Key
    F TROOP; The Great Indian Uprising
    GILLIGAN'S ISLAND
    IRONSIDE; The Picture Frame Frame-Up
    MONKEES, THE; Who's Got the Button?
    MUNSTERS, THE and The Great Camera Caper
            The Last Resort

Jones, Raymond F.; STORIES OF GREAT PHYSICIANS
    VOYAGE TO THE BOTTOM OF THE SEA

Keith, Brandon; GREEN HORNET, THE; The Case of the Disappearing Doctor
    I SPY; Message From Moscow
    MAN FROM U.N.C.L.E., THE
        The Affair of the Gentle Sabateur
        The Affair of the Gunrunner's Gold

Kenny, Kathryn; TRIXIE BELDEN®
            and The Marshland Mystery
            and The Missing Heiress
            and The Mysterious Code
            and The Mystery of the Blinking Eye
            and The Black Jacket Mystery
            and The Happy Valley Mystery
            and The Mystery at Bob-White Cave
            and The Mystery of the Emeralds
            and The Mystery on Cobbett's Island
            and The Mystery On the Mississippi

Ketchum, Philip; WYATT EARP

King, Frank; NINA AND SKEEZIX; (of "Gasoline Alley"), The Problem of the Lost Ring

Kirby, Jean; NURSES THREE; First Assignment, A Penny Scott Story

Laflin, Jack; THROW THE LONG BOMB

Lawson, Patrick; MORE THAN COURAGE

Lee, Wayne C.; BAT MASTERSON

Lewis, Francine; POLLY FRENCH, of Whitford High
            Takes Charge
            and The Surprising Stranger

Lloyd, Hugh; HAL KEEN; Hermit of Gordon's Creek

London, Jack; CALL OF THE WILD, THE

Lyle, Mel; POWER BOYS Adventure, A; The Mystery of the Burning Ocean
        The Mystery of the Double Kidnapping
        The Mystery of the Flying Skeleton
        The Mystery of the Haunted Skyscraper
        The Mystery of the Million Dollar Penny
        The Mystery of the Vanishing Lady

Martin, Edgar; BOOTS and The Mystery of the Unlucky Vase

Martin, Marcia; DONNA PARKER, A Spring To Remember
            At Cherrydale
            In Hollywood
            Mystery at Arawak
            On Her Own
            Special Agent
            Takes A Giant Step

Martinek, Frank V.; DON WINSLOW And The Scorpion's Stronghold

McDonnell, Jinny KIM ALDRICH MYSTERY, A Miscalculated Risk
            Silent Partner

McGill, Jerry; RED RYDER and The Riddle of the Roaring Range
            and the Thunder Trail

Mendel, Jo; TUCKERS, THE; The Cottage Holiday
            Trouble On Valley View
            The Special Secret

Meridith, Nicolete; MILESTONE SUMMER

Merrill, Anna Darby; MARY LEE'S FRIEND

Messick, Dale; BRENDA STARR; Girl Reporter

Myers, Barlow; CHAMPIONS ALL THE WAY;
    Real Life Stories of Outstanding Men and Women in The World of Sports
    HAVE GUN, WILL TRAVEL
    JANET LENNON; Adventure at Two Rivers
            and The Angels
            At Camp Calamity
    RESTLESS GUN, THE
    WALT DISNEY'S ANNETTE; Mystery at Medicine Wheel

Michelson, Florence B.; DEFIANT HEART, THE

Middleton, Don; ROY ROGERS; The Gopher Creek Gunman

Miller, Snowden; GENE AUTRY; Badmen of Broken Bow;
            ROY ROGERS; Raiders of Sawtooth Ridge
            Outlaws of Sundown Valley
            And the Rimrod Renegades

Mosley, Zack; SMILIN' JACK; and The Daredevil Girl
    Pilot

Murray, Michael; TIMBER TRAIL RIDERS; The Long
    Trail North
        The Luck of Black Diamond
        The Mystery of the Hollywood Horse
        The Texas Tenderfoot
        The Mysterious Dude

Nesbit, Troy; TROY NESBIT
        Sand Dune Pony
        The Diamond Cave Mystery
        The Forest Fire Mystery
        The Indian Mummy Mystery
        The Jinx of Payrock Canyon
        The Mystery at Rustler's Fort
WAGON TRAIN
FURY; The Mystery at Trapper's Hole

Newman, Paul S.; GUNSMOKE; Showdown On Front
    Street

Olney, Ross R.; DRAG STRIP DANGER

Patten, Lewis B.; GENE AUTRY and The Ghost Riders

Pearl, Jack; GARRISON'S GORILLAS; and The Fear
    Formula
    INVADERS, THE; Dam of Death
    SPACE EAGLE, THE; Operation Doomsday
        Operation Star Voyage

Poe, Edgar Allan; TALES OF EDGAR ALLAN POE

Porter, Gene Stratton; FRECKLES

Powell, Talmage; CELLAR TEAM
    MISSION: IMPOSSIBLE; The Priceless Particle
    MISSION: IMPOSSIBLE; The Money Explosion
    THING IN B-3, THE; A Tale of the Supernatural

Pyle, Howard; ROBIN HOOD

Radford, Ruby Lorraine; KITTY CARTER; Canteen
    Girl
    PEGGY PARKER; Girl Inventor
    SANDRA of The Girl Orchestra
    SYLVIA SANDERS and the Tangled Web

Rathjen, Carl Henry; LAND OF THE GIANTS; Flight
    of Fear
    SADDLE PATROL
    HOT ROD ROAD

Reynolds, Mack; STAR TREK; Mission To Horatius

Rice, Alice Hegan; MRS. WIGGS OF THE CABBAGE
    PATCH

Ritchie, Rita; BICYCLES NORTH; A Mystery On
    Wheels
    SILVER SEVEN, THE

Rivers, Jim; ROY ROGERS and The Enchanted
    Canyon

Roberts, Suzanne; SPIRIT TOWN

Robinson, Kathleen; WHEN DEBBIE DARED

Robinson, Mudd, Sayers & Gogolak; PLAYERS'
    CHOICE; Great Tales of the Gridiron

Rockwood, Roy; FIVE THOUSAND MILES UNDER
    GROUND
    LOST ON THE MOON; In Quest of the Field of
        Diamonds
    ON A TORN-AWAY WORLD; The Captives of the
        Great Earthquake

Rogers, Lela E.; GINGER ROGERS; The Riddle of the
    Scarlet Cloak

Rowe, Viola; TRUE TO YOU

Roy, Lillian; POLLY BREWSTER; In New York
        Polly of Pebbly Pit

Saunders, Marshall; BEAUTIFUL JOE

Savage, Blake; RIP FOSTER
        Assignment In Space with
        Rides the Gray Planet

Schroeder, Doris; ANNIE OAKLEY In Danger at Diablo
    BEVERLY HILLBILLIES, THE
        The Saga of Wildcat Creek
    LASSIE; Forbidden Valley
    LENNON SISTERS, THE;
        The Secret of Holiday Island
    PATTY DUKE
        and The Adventure of the Chinese Junk
        and The Mystery Mansion;
    RIN TIN TIN and The Call To Danger
    WALT DISNEY'S ANNETTE and The Mystery At
        Moonstone Bay Sierra Summer
        The Desert Inn Mystery
    WALT DISNEY'S SPIN AND MARTY; Trouble At
Triple-R

Schwaljie, Marjorie; MYSTERY AT RED TOP HILL

Seton, Ernest Thompson; WILD ANIMALS I HAVE
    KNOWN
    BIOGRAPHY OF A GRIZZLY AND LOBO, THE

Sewell, Anna; BLACK BEAUTY

Sherwood, Elmer; BUFFALO BILL; The Boys' Friend

Sidney, Margaret; FIVE LITTLE PEPPERS and How
    They Grew

Smith, Carl W.; QUIZ KIDS and The Crazy Question
    Mystery

Smith, Carl; RED RYDER and The Secret of the
    Lucky Mine

Snell, Roy J.; JANE WITHERS; The Phantom Violin;
NORMA KENT OF THE WACS
SALLY SCOTT OF THE WAVES

Snow, Dorothea J.; CHARMED CIRCLE, THE
CIRCUS BOY; Under the Big Top
War On Wheels
LASSIE; Mystery At Blackberry Bog
The Secret of Summer
THAT CERTAIN GIRL
WALT DISNEY'S TOBY TYLER

Spyri, Johanna; HEIDI

Stamm, Russell; INVISIBLE SCARLET O'NEIL

Stevenson, Robert Louis; KIDNAPPED
TREASURE ISLAND

Strong, Charles; LASSIE; Treasure Hunter

Thomas, H.C.;
A BOY FIGHTER WITH ANDREW JACKSON
A BOY SAILOR WITH JOHN PAUL JONES
NOAH CARR, YANKEE FIREBRAND

Tompkins, Walker A.; ROY ROGERS and The Ghost
of Mystery Rancho

Tritten, Charles; HEIDI Grows Up

Twain, Mark; HUCKLEBERRY FINN
TOM SAWYER

Various; A BATCH OF THE BEST; Stories For Girls
ADVENTURE CALLING
BLUE BOOK OF CHILDREN'S STORIES, THE
CHRISTMAS STORIES
FAMOUS FAIRY TALES
FAVORITE STORIES; A Collection of the Best-
loved Tales of Childhood
GOLDEN PRIZE and Other Stories About Horses
MORE TALES TO TREMBLE BY
MOTHER GOOSE
NURSES WHO LED THE WAY, Real Life Stories
of Courageous Women in an Exciting Profession
SCIENCE FICTION ADVENTURE FROM WAY OUT
SEVEN GREAT DETECTIVE STORIES
STAND BY FOR ADVENTURE
TEN TALES CALCULATED TO GIVE YOU
SHUDDERS

Wagner, Sharon; GYPSY FROM NOWHERE

Walker, Holly Beth; MEG and
The Disappearing Diamonds
The Ghost of Hidden Springs

The Mystery of the Black Magic Cave
The Secret of the Witch's Stairway
The Treasure Nobody Saw

Walsh and DaGradi; WALT DISNEY'S BEDKNOBS
AND BROOMSTICKS

Warner, Frank A.; BOBBY BLAKE; At Bass Cove or
the Hunt for the Motor Boat Gem
At Rockledge School

Washburn, Jan; FAMILY NAME, THE

Webb, Robert N.; CHALLENGE OF ICE; Real Life
Stories of Polar Explorers
WALT DISNEY'S HANS BRINKER; or The Silver
Skates

Weiss, Joan Talmage; DORY BOY
KENNY AND HIS ANIMAL FRIENDS

Wellman, Alice; TAMMY; Adventure In Hollywood

Wells, H.G.; WAR OF THE WORLDS

Westover, Russ; TILLIE THE TOILER and The
Masquerading Duchess

Whitehill, Dorothy; JOY AND PAM At Brookside

Wiggin, Kate Douglas; REBECCA OF SUNNYBROOK
FARM

Winfield, Arthur M.; ROVER BOYS THE
On Treasure Isle
In Southern Waters
On the Plains

Winterbotham, R.R.; JOYCE OF THE SECRET
SQUADRON; A Captain Midnight Adventure

Wise, Winifred E.; "MINNOW" VAIL

Wyatt, George; BRAINS BENTON MYSTERY, A
The Case of the Counterfeit Coin
The Case of the Painted Dragon
The Case of the Roving Rolls
The Case of the Stolen Dummy

Wyss, Johann R.; SWISS FAMILY ROBINSON, THE

Young, Chic; BLONDIE
and Dagwood's Adventure In Magic
Dagwood's Snapshot Clue
Dagwood's Secret Service

DOLLS, FIGURES & TEDDY BEARS

2079	**Barbie** Doll Fashion, Volume I, Eames	$24.95
3957	**Barbie** Exclusives, Rana	$18.95
4557	**Barbie**, The First 30 Years, Deutsch	$24.95
3310	**Black Dolls**, Book I, Perkins	$17.95
3810	**Chatty Cathy** Dolls, Lewis	$15.95
4559	Collectible **Action Figures**, 2nd Ed., Manos	$17.95
1529	Collector's Encyclopedia of **Barbie** Dolls, DeWein/Ashabraner	$19.95
2211	Collector's Encyclopedia of **Madame Alexander Dolls**, 1965-1990, Smith	$24.95
4863	Collector's Encyclopedia of **Vogue Dolls**, Stover/Izen	$29.95
4861	Collector's Guide to **Tammy**, Sabulis/Weglewski	$18.95
3967	Collector's Guide to **Trolls**, Peterson	$19.95
1799	**Effanbee Dolls**, Smith	$19.95
4571	**Liddle Kiddles**, Langford	$18.95
3826	Story of **Barbie**, Westenhouser	$19.95
1513	**Teddy Bears & Steiff** Animals, Mandel	$9.95
1817	**Teddy Bears & Steiff** Animals, 2nd Series, Mandel	$19.95
2084	**Teddy Bears, Annalee's & Steiff** Animals, 3rd Series, Mandel	$19.95
1808	Wonder of **Barbie**, Manos	$9.95
1430	World of **Barbie** Dolls, Manos	$9.95
4880	World of **Raggedy Ann Collectibles**, Avery	$24.95

TOYS, MARBLES & CHRISTMAS COLLECTIBLES

3427	**Advertising Character** Collectibles, Dotz	$17.95
2333	Antique & Collectible **Marbles**, 3rd Ed., Grist	$9.95
3827	Antique & Collector's **Toys**, 1870–1950, Longest	$24.95
3956	Baby Boomer **Games**, Identification & Value Guide, Polizzi	$24.95
4934	**Breyer Animal** Collector's Guide, Identification and Values, Browell	$19.95
1514	Character **Toys** & Collectibles, Longest	$19.95
1750	Character **Toys** & Collector's, 2nd Series, Longest	$19.95
3717	**Christmas** Collectibles, 2nd Edition, Whitmyer	$24.95
4976	**Christmas** Ornaments, Lights & Decorations, Johnson	$24.95
4737	**Christmas** Ornaments, Lights & Decorations, Vol. II, Johnson	$24.95
4739	**Christmas** Ornaments, Lights & Decorations, Vol. III, Johnson	$24.95
2338	Collector's Encyclopedia of **Disneyana**, Longest, Stern	$24.95
4958	Collector's Guide to **Battery Toys**, Hultzman	$19.95
4639	Collector's Guide to **Diecast Toys** & Scale Models, Johnson	$19.95
4566	Collector's Guide to **Tootsietoys**, 2nd Ed, Richter	$19.95
3436	Grist's Big Book of **Marbles**	$19.95
3970	Grist's Machine-Made & Contemporary **Marbles**, 2nd Ed.	$9.95
4723	**Matchbox Toys**, 2nd Ed., 1947 to 1996, Johnson	$18.95
4871	**McDonald's Collectibles**, Henriques/DuVall	$19.95
1540	**Modern Toys** 1930–1980, Baker	$19.95
3888	**Motorcycle Toys**, Antique & Contemporary, Gentry/Downs	$18.95
4953	Schroeder's Collectible **Toys**, Antique to Modern Price Guide, 4th Ed	$17.95
1886	Stern's Guide to **Disney** Collectibles	$14.95
2139	Stern's Guide to **Disney** Collectibles, 2nd Series	$14.95
3975	Stern's Guide to **Disney** Collectibles, 3rd Series	$18.95
28	**Toys**, Antique & Collectible, Longest	$14.95

JEWELRY, HATPINS, WATCHES & PURSES

	Antique & Collectible **Thimbles** & Accessories, Mathis	$19.95
	Antique **Purses**, Revised Second Ed., Holiner	$19.95
	Art Nouveau & Art Deco **Jewelry**, Baker	$9.95
	Collectible **Costume Jewelry**, Simonds	$24.95
	Collecting Antique **Stickpins**, Kerins	$16.95
	Collector's Ency. of **Compacts, Carryalls & Face Powder Boxes**, Mueller	$24.95
	Costume Jewelry, A Practical Handbook & Value Guide, Rezazadeh	$24.95
716	Fifty Years of Collectible **Fashion Jewelry**, 1925-1975, Baker	$19.95
1424	**Hatpins** & Hatpin Holders, Baker	$9.95
1181	100 Years of Collectible **Jewelry**, 1850-1950, Baker	$9.95
2348	20th Century Fashionable Plastic **Jewelry**, Baker	$19.95
3830	Vintage **Vanity Bags & Purses**, Gerson	$24.95

FURNITURE

1457	American **Oak** Furniture, McNerney	$9.95
3716	American **Oak** Furniture, Book II, McNerney	$12.95
1118	Antique **Oak** Furniture, Hill	$7.95
2132	Collector's Encyclopedia of **American** Furniture, Vol. I, Swedberg	$24.95
2271	Collector's Encyclopedia of **American** Furniture, Vol. II, Swedberg	$24.95
3720	Collector's Encyclopedia of **American** Furniture, Vol. III, Swedberg	$24.95
1755	Furniture of the **Depression Era**, Swedberg	$19.95
3906	**Heywood-Wakefield** Modern Furniture, Rouland	$18.95
1885	**Victorian** Furniture, Our American Heritage, McNerney	$9.95
3829	**Victorian** Furniture, Our American Heritage, Book II, McNerney	$9.95

INDIANS, GUNS, KNIVES, TOOLS, PRIMITIVES

1868	Antique **Tools**, Our American Heritage, McNerney	$9.95
1426	**Arrowheads** & Projectile Points, Hothem	$7.95
2279	**Indian** Artifacts of the Midwest, Hothem	$14.95
3885	**Indian** Artifacts of the Midwest, Book II, Hothem	$16.95
4724	Modern **Guns**, Identification & Values, 11th Ed., Quertermous	$12.95
2164	**Primitives**, Our American Heritage, McNerney	$9.95
1759	**Primitives**, Our American Heritage, Series II, McNerney	$14.95
4730	Standard **Knife** Collector's Guide, 3rd Ed., Ritchie & Stewart	$12.95 .

PAPER COLLECTIBLES & BOOKS

4633	**Big Little Books**, A Collector's Reference & Value Guide, Jacobs	$18.95
4710	Collector's Guide to **Children's Books**, 1850 to 1950, Jones	$18.95
1441	Collector's Guide to **Post Cards**, Wood	$9.95
2081	Guide to Collecting **Cookbooks**, Allen	$14.95
2080	Price Guide to **Cookbooks & Recipe Leaflets**, Dickinson	$9.95
3973	**Sheet Music** Reference & Price Guide, 2nd Ed., Pafik & Guiheen	$19.95
4654	**Victorian Trade Cards**, Historical Reference & Value Guide, Cheadle	$19.95
4733	**Whitman Juvenile Books**, Brown	$17.95

OTHER COLLECTIBLES

2269	Antique **Brass & Copper** Collectibles, Gaston	$16.95
1880	Antique **Iron**, McNerney	$9.95
3872	Antique **Tins**, Dodge	$24.95
1128	**Bottle** Pricing Guide, 3rd Ed., Cleveland	$7.95
3718	Collectible **Aluminum**, Grist	$16.95
4560	Collectible **Cats**, An Identification & Value Guide, Book II, Fyke	$19.95
4852	Collectible **Compact Disc** Price Guide 2, Cooper	$17.95
2018	Collector's Encyclopedia of **Granite Ware**, Greguire	$24.95
3430	Collector's Encyclopedia of **Granite Ware**, Book II, Greguire	$24.95
3879	Collector's Guide to Antique **Radios**, 3rd Ed., Bunis	$18.95
1916	Collector's Guide to **Art Deco**, Gaston	$14.95
4933	Collector's Guide to **Bookends**, Identification & Values, Kuritzky	$19.95
3880	Collector's Guide to **Cigarette Lighters**, Flanagan	$17.95
4887	Collector's Guide to **Creek Chub Lures** & Collectibles, Smith	$24.95
3966	Collector's Guide to **Inkwells**, Identification & Values, Badders	$18.95
3881	Collector's Guide to **Novelty Radios**, Bunis/Breed	$18.95
3730	Collector's Guide to **Transistor Radios**, Bunis	$15.95
4864	Collector's Guide to **Wallace Nutting Pictures**, Ivankovich	$18.95
1629	**Doorstops**, Identification & Values, Bertoia	$9.95
3968	**Fishing Lure** Collectibles, Murphy/Edmisten	$24.95
4867	**Flea Market Trader**, 11th Ed., Huxford	$9.95
4945	**G-Men and FBI Toys**, Whitworth	$18.95
3819	**General Store Collectibles**, Wilson	$24.95
2215	**Goldstein's Coca-Cola** Collectibles	$16.95
2216	**Kitchen Antiques**, 1790–1940, McNerney	$14.95
4950	The **Lone Ranger**, Collector's Reference & Value Guide, Felbinger	$18.95
2026	**Railroad** Collectibles, 4th Ed., Baker	$14.95
1632	**Salt & Pepper Shakers**, Guarnaccia	$9.95
1888	**Salt & Pepper Shakers** II, Guarnaccia	$14.95
2220	**Salt & Pepper Shakers** III, Guarnaccia	$14.95
3443	**Salt & Pepper Shakers** IV, Guarnaccia	$18.95
2096	**Silverplated Flatware**, Revised 4th Edition, Hagan	$14.95
1922	Standard **Old Bottle** Price Guide, Sellari	$14.95
3892	**Toy & Miniature Sewing Machines**, Thomas	$18.95
3828	Value Guide to **Advertising Memorabilia**, Summers	$18.95
3977	Value Guide to **Gas Station** Memorabilia, Summers	$24.95
4877	Vintage **Bar Ware**, Visakay	$24.95
4935	The W.F. Cody **Buffalo Bill** Collector's Guide with Values, Wojtowicz	$24.95
4879	**Wanted to Buy**, 6th Edition	$9.95

GLASSWARE & POTTERY

4929	**American Art Pottery**, 1880 – 1950, Sigafoose	$24.95
4938	Collector's Encyclopedia of **Depression Glass**, 13th Ed., Florence	$19.95
5040	Collector's Encyclopedia of **Fiesta**, 8th Ed., Huxford	$19.95
4946	Collector's Encyclopedia of **Howard Pierce Porcelain**, Dommel	$24.95
1358	Collector's Encyclopedia of **McCoy Pottery**, Huxford	$19.95
2339	Collector's Guide to **Shawnee Pottery**, Vanderbilt	$19.95
1523	Colors in **Cambridge Glass**, National Cambridge Society	$19.95
2275	**Czechoslovakian Glass** and Collectibles, Barta	$16.95
3725	**Fostoria**, Pressed, Blown & Hand Molded Shapes, Kerr	$24.95
4726	**Red Wing Art Pottery**, 1920s – 1960s, Dollen	$19.95

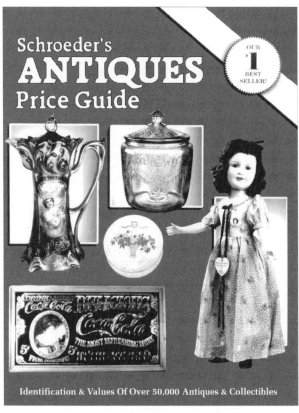